RICHARD FAWCETT

·SCOTTISH MEDIEVAL· CHURCHES

AN INTRODUCTION TO THE ECCLESIASTICAL ARCHITECTURE
OF THE 12TH TO 16TH CENTURIES
IN THE CARE OF THE SECRETARY OF STATE FOR SCOTLAND.

Let us explore the ruin'd Abbeys Choir;
Its fretted roof and windows of rich Tracery,
The Sculptur'd Tombs o'ergrown with shrubs and brambles,
'Midst broken arches, graves and gloomy vaults,
Or view the Castle of Some Ancient Thane
Its Hall, its Dungeons and Embattled ⸍
Mantled with Ivy, —

Francis Grose, Antiꝗ

HISTORIC BUILDINGS AND MONUMENTS DIRECTORATE

Scottish Development Department

EDINBURGH
HER MAJESTY'S STATIONERY OFFICE

Contents

Note

The church plans are drawn to a uniform scale of 1.8 cm to 15 metres.

The plans of monastic buildings are drawn to a scale of 1.8 cm to 15 metres.

The sketches of capitals and window tracery are not to scale.

Designed by J Cairns HMSO/GD

HER MAJESTY'S STATIONERY OFFICE

Government Bookshops

13a Castle Street, Edinburgh EH2 3AR
49 High Holborn, London WC1V 6HB
Brazennose Street, Manchester M60 8AS
Southey House, Wine Street, Bristol BS1 2BQ
258 Broad Street, Birmingham B1 2HE
80 Chichester Street, Belfast BT1 4JY

Government publications are also available through booksellers

Crown Copyright 1985
First published 1985

ISBN 0 11 492385 X

Preface

FEW would dispute that those medieval churches which have come down to us in Scotland are amongst the most beautiful buildings we possess, and simply to walk through them can be a great source of pleasure. However, since they were produced at times, and in response to needs which may now seem remote from us, it can be very difficult to understand why these buildings were raised in the form we see. This difficulty is all the greater when the churches are in a state of ruination, however much that ruination may enhance their picturesque appeal.

It is the aim of this small book to overcome some of this sense of remoteness by providing visitors to the medieval churches which are in State care with information which will help them to understand what they see. The organisation of the medieval Church is briefly described, along with the functions and requirements which dictated the way in which the buildings were laid out, and the manner in which they were used. Additionally, by offering a short account of changing architectural fashions over the four and half centuries between the reorganisation of the Scottish Church in the early twelfth century and the Reformation in 1560, it is hoped that visitors will be assisted to derive a further dimension of pleasure from their tours of these most delightful buildings.

In considering the ecclesiastical architecture of Scotland, it should be remembered that politically, culturally and linguistically the area had earlier been greatly divided. South of the Forth-Clyde basin were the British peoples, although from the mid-seventh century onwards the eastern half of this region was increasingly dominated by the Anglian kingdom of Northumbria. The western Highlands were occupied by the Scots of neighbouring Ireland, and became part of the kingdom of Dalriada, whilst the Picts occupied much of central, eastern and northern Scotland. The process of welding these diverse elements together began with the unification of Dalriada and Pictland under Kenneth MacAlpin in 843, and continued under the kings of the Canmore dynasty. However, the occupation of parts of the northern and western seaboards by Vikings from the ninth century onwards, along with the fluid state of the boundary with England for much of the middle ages, meant that Scotland's kings only attained full control of what is now Scotland towards the end of the period covered by this book.

As far as possible references are to buildings in the care of the State, but, since certain types of ecclesiastical structures are inadequately illustrated within this group, other churches are also mentioned where necessary.

Opposite.
Melrose Abbey choir.

A corbel at Melrose Abbey.

THE HISTORICAL BACKGROUND

The Cathedrals

Early Foundations

A cathedral is the church in which a bishop places his seat (*cathedra*), as the symbol of his spiritual authority, and it is thus the principal church within the territorial area, known as a diocese, over which he presides. It is thought that the earliest attempts to form dioceses in Scotland may have taken place in the early fifth century, under the leadership of St Ninian. However, there is much uncertainty about this, and, following the advent of the Irish missionary monks in Scotland in 563, any cathedral centres then existing seem to have been transformed into monasteries, with abbots rather than bishops in control. It was probably only after a Synod (meeting of Church leaders) at Whitby, in 663, determined that the organisation of the Roman Church should replace that of the Celtic Church that bishops began to play a more significant role. Surviving evidence suggests that, from at least the eighth century onwards, a pattern of dioceses began to emerge which may have covered much of Scotland, although the picture is one of frequent change.

The Twelfth Century Reorganisation

By the early twelfth century it appears that the rudimentary diocesan organisation of the Church had decayed, and it was largely due to the Canmore dynasty of Scottish kings that the system was re-established on a more effective basis. A leading part in this was taken by David I who, even before his

1. A depiction of St Ninian in a fifteenth century Scottish service book. The saint is here shown in the vestments which would be worn by a late medieval bishop when celebrating mass. (*Edinburgh University Library, MS 42*)

2. A decorated initial from a charter of 1159 granted to Kelso Abbey, which shows David I (on the left) with his grandson, Malcom IV. Although this charter dates from after David I's death, it is possible that the artist has made some attempt to represent the likeness of the king. (*From the collection of the Duke of Roxburghe*)

succession to the throne in 1124, had revived the ancient diocese of Glasgow, which was within the area over which his elder brother, Alexander I, allowed him control.

David I was probably the most devout monarch to occupy the Scottish throne, and his wish to see the Church properly established within his kingdom was undoubtedly prompted largely by his own deeply held religious faith. Yet, as a prince who had spent many years at the English court of his brother-in-law, Henry I, and as a holder of extensive lands in England through marriage to a great heiress, David had early come to realise that his own country was out of line with the rest of feudal Europe in many respects. His efforts for the Church must thus also be seen as part of a far-reaching policy to bring Scotland into greater conformity with northern Europe, and to impose more effective government on those outlying parts of his kingdom which might still regard themselves as being beyond royal control.

Thus, in addition to re-establishing several of the older dioceses, amongst which St Andrews had already gained pre-eminence, he was also responsible for forming a diocese of Caithness in the far north, in an attempt to reduce Norse control over the area. (The adjacent diocese of Orkney was still firmly Norse and, along with the diocese of the Isles, was placed under the authority of Trondheim in Norway.) Conversely, in the far south-west of the country the diocese of Galloway, based on Whithorn, was re-established by the local magnate, Fergus, and was to remain outside the main enclave of the Scottish Church until the mid-fourteenth century.

In order to counter the claims of the Archbishops of York to supremacy over the whole Scottish Church, it was David I's aim to have an archbishop at St Andrews. However, although the separate identity of the Scottish Church within the fold of Catholic Europe was generally recognised by the late twelfth century, it was only in 1472 that St Andrews eventually became an archdiocese, with Glasgow being accorded similar status twenty years later.

Of Scotland's thirteen medieval cathedrals two of those which remain fully in use, Dunblane and Glasgow, are in State care, as are parts of Aberdeen, Brechin and Dunkeld. Also in State care are the ruins of Elgin, Fortrose, St Andrews and Whithorn cathedrals.

The Cathedral Clergy

As the most important churches of the kingdom it was fitting that the cathedrals should be seen to give seemly expression to the daily round of religious observance, but to do this it was first necessary for them to be supported by an appropriately constituted body of clergy. For guidance in this the Scottish bishops naturally tended to look to England, where cathedrals were organised in two different ways, both of which were to be copied in Scotland. Either there was a community of monks or of regular canons (regular means they lived according to a monastic rule, a *regula*), or they had a staff of priests known as secular canons (in this sense "secular" means non-monastic). In either case the canons or monks formed the body known as the chapter, which was corporately responsible for the administration of the cathedral and its possessions, as well as for providing an unbroken round of religious services. Since bishops were often employed in matters of State and might be absent for long periods from their cathedral churches, the chapters tended to assume a dominant role in the running of the cathedrals, and might even grow to resent what they saw as interference by bishops in their own areas of responsibility.

The type of cathedral chapter with either monks or regular canons, was found at many of the major English cathedrals — including Canterbury — although it was uncommon in the rest of Europe. In Scotland only the cathedrals of St Andrews and Whithorn were of this type, and they were served by priories of Augustinian and Premonstratensian canons respectively (see pages 17-18). In these priories the bishop was nominally regarded as occupying the place of the abbot, the head of the community, although the effective head was a prior, who also assumed the role played by the dean in the chapters of secular canons. The daily life of the communities of regular canons was in most respects the same as that of the other monastic houses, which will be considered below (see page 20).

When a cathedral was served by secular canons, each canon enjoyed a separate income known as a prebend, as well as certain shared benefits, and each lived independently with his own household. Amongst the canons there were usually four officers of particular importance, who were known as the dignitaries: the dean, who was their administrative head; the precentor, who was in charge of the cathedral music; the chancellor, who was the

businessman of the Chapter; the treasurer, who was responsible for the precious possessions of the cathedral body. An example of a late medieval canon's residence, possibly that of the precentor, still partly survives in the mis-named 'Bishop's House' at Elgin. Since canons could not always be in residence at their cathedrals—but also because it later became common for many to regard their prebend simply as a source of income involving few duties on their part—they were expected to provide substitutes for themselves to ensure the continuity of religious observance. These substitutes were usually known as vicars choral, and had to be paid for and provided with choir vestments by their canons.

At the time the Scottish cathedrals were first re-established many of them were so poorly endowed that they could afford no more than a minimal chapter of canons, but progressively sufficient funds were found, often by diverting the endowments of parish churches, to allow many of our cathedrals to support an adequate complement. Glasgow, for example, eventually had thirty-two canons, although the final number at the much poorer cathedral of Brechin was probably no more than fourteen. Since a bishop had no place in his cathedral's chapter in his own right, the head of which was the dean, his relationship with the chapter might be somewhat anomalous. As a way round this, at several Scottish cathedrals the bishop was also appointed to one of the canonries, and thus had a voice in chapter along with the other canons. Nevertheless, relations between a bishop and his cathedral's chapter might often be fraught with difficulty because of conflicts over jurisdiction within the cathedral body.

The Religious Life of the Cathedrals

The medieval liturgy was very rich and, particularly at important festivals, much of each day was occupied by services. As with the constitution of the cathedral clergy, so with the form of the religious observance, Scotland tended to look to England for guidance in the twelfth and thirteenth centuries, and in England it was the variant on the basic Roman rite developed for use at Salisbury cathedral (known consequently as the Sarum Rite) which was prevalent. The use of this rite at Elgin, for example, was adopted in 1242. Nevertheless, it is clear that Scotland was sufficiently independent to make adaptations where these seemed appropriate, particularly where celebrations for local saints were concerned, and, after the breach

3. The manse of one of the canons of Elgin Cathedral. Although often known as the 'Bishop's House', this manse was possibly that of the precentor. Its main block is extensively ruined, but the adjoining stair tower and north wing survive to their full height, and show that the manse would have formed a most imposing residence, in keeping with the high social standing of its occupant. It bears the date 1557.

with England at the end of the thirteenth century, there is also growing evidence of the importation of new ideas from the continent. Under the patronage of James IV, Bishop Elphinstone of Aberdeen attempted to formulate a liturgy "efter our awin Scottis Use", which culminated in the publication of the Aberdeen Breviary in 1510.

The daily round of services varied according to the time of year and the importance of the particular day, but the basic routine was similar to that of the monastic churches, and consisted chiefly of a series of seven services known as 'hours', made up largely of psalms, readings and prayers (see page 20). In addition, the celebration of the high mass was a principal focal point of the day, although there was a growing tendency to celebrate ever more masses with an accompanying need for increased numbers of altars. Most of these masses were essentially private celebrations by the priests attached to the cathedral, but large numbers of masses were also paid for by individuals, or by groups such as craft guilds, as part of the endeavour to ensure salvation of their souls after death. In many cases additional priests would be provided specifically for that purpose, but in cathedrals those vicars choral who were ordained as priests might also welcome payment for celebrating additional masses as a means of augmenting their incomes.

The Planning of the Cathedrals

A cathedral served a dual function, and this was demonstrated by the way its building was laid out. It was primarily the church of a group of clergy which was responsible for performing an unbroken daily round of services with a dignity which would reflect the importance of the Church and its bishops. But, as the mother church of its particular diocese, it was also open to the lay folk, who would gather in large numbers on the greater feast days, or to venetrate the relics of a saint which might be preserved within the church. It should be added that, since the majority of Scottish cathedrals also acted as a parish church to their local communities, adequate provision for the lay folk was especially necessary.

Where possible a cathedral, like any other church, was set out on an axis from east to west, with the focus of the whole building, the high altar, at or near the east end. Provision for the canons who served the cathedral was made near to the altar, within a more or less architecturally distinct limb, known as the choir, whilst the lay folk were housed in a western limb known as the nave. In the larger cathedrals the structural division between the two parts might be emphasised by projecting lateral limbs, known as transepts, which accommodated additional altars and processional areas.

The main body of the choir was usually an elongated space with the ceremonial area around the high altar, known as the presbytery, towards its eastern end. To the west of the presbytery the bishop's throne and the stalls of the dignataries and canons ran along the side walls and returned across the end where the choir and nave were divided from each other by a screen. Well-preserved examples of such stalls survive in the cathedral of Dunblane, although they are no longer in their original position. The benches of the vicars choral usually ran in front of the canons' stalls. At

4. The celebration of high mass in a major church. The celebrating priest with attendant deacon and subdeacon are at the high altar, behind which rises a magnificent reredos. Canons and chaplains kneel close to the altar or occupy the richly carved stalls down the sides of the choir. Certain favoured lay folk are also allowed into the choir, but the rest peer through the rood screen which separates the nave from the choir. An organ stands on the loft above the screen. (Chantilly, Musée Condé MS 65 f 158r)

some cathedrals, including Fortrose, Dunkeld, and Dunblane, the choir was never more than a rectangle in plan, although usually with some form of projection on its northern side to house ancillary offices such as the chapter house (the meeting room of the chapter), the sacristy (where the priests prepared for the services) and perhaps also a treasury. At the cathedrals of Elgin (fig 10), St Andrews and Whithorn, however, the choir was flanked by processional aisles, which opened into the central space through tall arcades and had chapels at their eastern ends. Sometimes these aisles gave access to a feretory behind the high altar, where the shrine of a saint was displayed for the veneration of pilgrims. The type of plan seen at St Andrews, in which the presbytery continues beyond the flanking aisles, was repeated at a number of abbeys. It appears to have originated soon after 1108 in the Nottinghamshire collegiate church of Southwell, and was afterwards used in several northern English churches, such as the Augustinian priories of Lanercost and Cartmel, as well as in Scotland.

At mid-thirteenth century Glasgow an even more elaborate plan was employed, with an eastern aisle (known as an ambulatory), behind the high altar, and

5. Three of the surviving canopied stalls at Dunblane Cathedral. The seats are lifted to reveal the misericords on which the canons could rest during the long parts of the services which required standing. The misericord on the right bears the arms of one of the three bishops of the Chisholm family who occupied the see between 1487 and 1569, and probably refers to James Chisholm, who was bishop from 1487 to 1526.

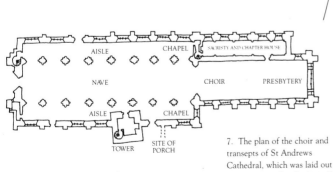

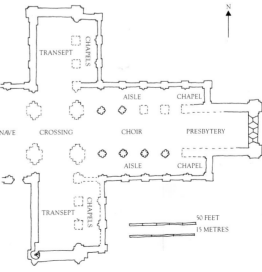

6. The plan of Dunblane Cathedral, which is similar to several other Scottish cathedrals of middle rank in its modest scale, and the absence of aisles to the choir.

7. The plan of the choir and transepts of St Andrews Cathedral, which was laid out on a very grand scale. A similar plan was employed for several abbey churches, albeit on a smaller scale, and the choir of Elgin Cathedral was eventually enlarged to this form after 1270 (see fig 10).

8. The plan of Glasgow Cathedral, which is unusual for the way in which its main body is contained within a single rectangle, and for the aisle which extends around three sides of the choir.

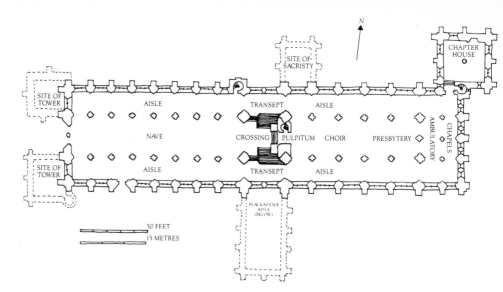

9. Glasgow Cathedral, viewed from the south-east. The thirteenth century aisled choir, with its eastern aisle and row of chapels, is particularly prominent in this view because of the way in which it is raised above a crypt. The non-projecting transepts which separate choir and nave represent a modification of the original intentions, since the crypt of a very large south transept was laid out in the thirteenth century. This crypt was only eventually completed by Archbishop Blackadder at the turn of the fifteenth and sixteenth centuries, however, and was never carried up beyond that level.

a series of chapels beyond. This type of plan appears to have originated with the Cistercian order of monks (see page 16) as a simple means of housing a large number of altars. Cîteaux itself had been rebuilt in this form in the second half of the twelfth century, and a variant was built at Abbey Dore in Herefordshire. Glasgow was yet more remarkable for having a spacious crypt below its choir, a distinction shared only by Whithorn amongst Scottish cathedrals. These crypts were necessitated by the fall of the land, although a requirement of space for the cults of local saints — Mungo (or Kentigern) at Glasgow and Ninian at Whithorn — helped to govern the choice of sites and the consequent two-level arrangement.

Less variety of planning was shown in cathedral naves, where the chief requirement was a sufficiency of space to accommodate the laity and the furnishings, such as altars, a font and a pulpit, necessary to meet their needs. The chief of these needs was for one or more principal altars, which would have been placed before the screen closing off the west end of the choir from general access. This screen was known as the rood screen, because of the great rood (crucifix) which was placed above it, and in some cases there was a second more solid screen between it and the choir, which was known as a pulpitum, an example of which survives at Glasgow. Cathedrals were further compartmented by other screens around the large number of additional altars which were progressively founded throughout the building. At St Andrews, for example, there were eventually about twenty altars in the nave alone, whilst in Glasgow's nave there were about twelve, most of which were placed in the flanking aisles. The majority

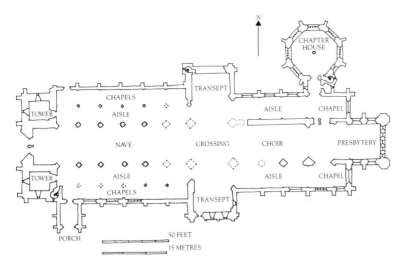

10. The plan of Elgin Cathedral, which is unique amongst Scottish Cathedrals in having an outer rank of chapels running along each aisle of the nave. A similar row of chapels was to be built along the south flank of Melrose Abbey, however, and such outer chapels were less systematically added to a number of parish churches.

of cathedrals had one or more aisles opening off the nave, although at Elgin there were two on each side in its final form, with the outer aisles sub-divided into chapels. At Whithorn, however, the nave remained aisle-less throughout its history, and must have presented a marked contrast to the rather more elaborate choir of the canons.

Architectural prominence was given to most cathedrals by the construction of towers, usually at the western end of the nave or at the crossing of nave, choir and transepts. Aberdeen, Elgin and Glasgow had three towers each — two at the west end and one at the crossing — although none of these has retained its full complement. Brechin still has a pleasingly asymmetrical pair of towers at its western end, including one of Scotland's two originally free-standing round towers of Irish type. Dunblane and Dunkeld each have a single tower, the latter to one side of the west front and the former, which survives from an earlier building, projecting from the south nave aisle.

The Religious Houses

Early Monasticism

Once Christianity was no longer confined to small numbers, some of the more devout souls felt the need to live apart from the world, either as solitary individuals (as hermits) or with like-minded fellows (as monks). As early as the third and fourth centuries St Antony was giving the monastic ideal a more coherent form, and later leaders such as St Basil and John Cassian added to the tradition of thought which saw rejection of the world as the best path to salvation.

But the greatest individual contributor was St Benedict of Nursia who, at some date around 530, prepared a detailed rule for the monastic life of poverty, chastity and obedience for his community at Monte Cassino in southern Italy. Although based to a considerable extent on the writings of predecessors, its eminent good sense has provided the principal cornerstone for monastic life in the Christian West.

11. A depiction of St Benedict of Nursia (on the right), one of the most important fathers of western monasticism. This painting, which dates from the later eleventh century, shows the saint symbolically receiving a book about his life from its author, Desiderius, a later abbot of Benedict's own community at Monte Cassino. (Rome, Biblioteca Apostolica Vaticana, MS Vat Lat 1202 f 2r)

13

On the basis of the Venerable Bede's history of the early church in England and the neighbouring regions, it has been argued that monasticism was introduced into Scotland by St Ninian in the early fifth century. But it is now considered more likely that it was only with the arrival of St Columba from Ireland in 563, and the foundation of Iona two years later, that true monasticism — albeit of a distinctively Celtic form — was firmly established here. Many similar monasteries were soon founded throughout Scotland at the height of the missionary activity of the Irish saints, although the decision of the Synod of Whitby against the Celtic Church in 663, followed by Norse raids in the ninth and tenth centuries, was eventually to bring about the decline of most of them. By the time St Margaret married Malcolm Canmore, in about 1070, it is doubtful if Scotland possessed many recognisable monasteries with the exception of Iona. Most other communities at that time to which references survive were probably composed of secular priests, many of whom are known to have been Culdees (vassals of God), the successors of a movement to reform the clergy which had spread from Ireland to Scotland around the ninth century.

The Introduction of European Monasticism

As with the establishment of the diocesan system, it was largely due to the efforts of the more devout members of the Canmore dynasty that Scottish monasticism was brought into conformity with that of Europe. The individuals who were chiefly responsible were St Margaret herself and her sons, but above all David I, the third of her sons to succeed to the throne. One of Margaret's most significant actions was to enlist the help of Lanfranc, the Archbishop of Canterbury, who provided her with a group of Benedictine monks for the church she built at Dunfermline, where she had earlier married Malcolm III.

David I was a worthy follower of his mother, both before and after his succession to the throne in 1124. His lengthy residence in England, along with his natural piety, had allowed him to gain a profound knowledge of the varieties of monastic life which were emerging at a period of intense spiritual activity, although we know from Ailred of Rievaulx that he had a particular affection for the austere order of Cistercian monks. Before 1124 David was a patron of at least nine monasteries of different orders in both England and Scotland, and his generosity to his

Scottish foundations after that date was yet more marked — to an extent, indeed, that the resources of his poor kingdom could hardly afford. Additionally, with his encouragement, several of the greater magnates were themselves patrons of monasteries. Amongst the most active were those of Anglo-Norman origin whose settlement David had supported as part of his effort to bring Scotland more into line with Europe; but some of the semi-independent lords of Scotland's outlying regions also showed themselves to be open-handed to the religious orders — perhaps to demonstrate that they were the equals of the newcomers.

David's patronage coincided with a period when the monastic movement had reached one of its peaks of achievement and, although the momentum continued for some years after his death, it was perhaps inevitable that the monasteries should lose lay support as their initial fervour waned. From the 1230s attention was increasingly diverted to the friars, whose renewed emphasis on personal poverty, along with a fresh concern for lively preaching to the laity, attracted much popular support. Nevertheless, by the end of the thirteenth century most of the major foundations of religious houses of all kinds had already been made. Although the friars were to attract a second wave of attention towards the end of the Middle Ages, the laity were by then generally tending to seek other outlets for their pious munificence.

The Religious Orders

The Church, like any other living organism, has always been subject to periodic phases of decline and subsequent renewal and, although the sixteenth century Reformation was the most drastic of these efforts at renewal, there were others which had a major impact on the course of the Church's history. This rhythm of decline and renewal is probably more easily observed in the religious orders than elsewhere. As original aspirations inevitably become institutionalised, it is rare for there not to be a slackening of ideals and, indeed, only one religious order — that of the Carthusians — has been able to claim that it was 'never reformed because never deformed'. One of the most important phases of renewal came at the start of the period with which this small book is concerned, the twelfth century, but to understand the importance of this century for monasticism it is necessary to look briefly at what had happened previously.

Celtic Monasticism, as introduced at Iona and elsewhere by the Irish monks under Columba after 563, was a harsh and ascetic form of life. The monks, whose life had many of the characteristics of that of hermits, lived on isolated sites in individual cells scattered around a small communal oratory. The early fervour of the Irish monks, particularly under the stern leadership of Columbanus, had driven them to remarkable achievements of penetration as far afield as France, Italy and Switzerland. But from the later seventh century onwards the expansion of the more organised Benedictine monasticism forced them into retreat.

Benedictine Monasticism, as has been said, has its roots in the rule compiled about 530 for his own abbey at Monte Cassino, by St Benedict of Nursia. But St Benedict had no idea of establishing a network, or order, of related abbeys throughout Europe, all living according to the same rule. The wider adoption of his rule only came gradually, and the formation of a centrally organised order very much later still. An important figure in this process was another St Benedict, of Aniane, who in the ninth century attempted to impose reform on the monasteries within the lands of the Emperor Louis the Pious. The first real attempt to form an order of Benedictine monks, however, only came with the fourth Lateran Council of 1216 and that attempt was attended by limited success. By that time other orders of monasteries had been established which, whilst following the rule of St Benedict, demonstrated the benefits for discipline of more systematic organisation.

By the period that Scotland was beginning to revive monasticism within its borders the newer orders of monks were already making their impact felt, and so the proportion of unmodified Benedictine houses is relatively small. But of seven Benedictine abbeys or priories known to have existed the most important, Dunfermline, is in State care. (An abbey was a largely autonomous community of monks under the leadership of an abbot; a priory, under the leadership of a prior, was a smaller community which in some cases might be dependent on an abbey.)

The Cluniac Order represents one of the first attempts to revert to a purer form of Benedictine monasticism. The abbey of Cluny in Burgundy was founded in 909, and soon became so famous for its way of life that it was asked to provide guidance to

other abbeys, or to patrons who wished to found new monasteries. At first there was no intention of forming a separate order of monasteries within the Benedictine framework, dependent on Cluny itself. But this is what eventually emerged at the height of the abbey's fame, with the abbot of Cluny as head of the order, and the newly founded satellite monasteries initially having only a prior as their head. Of the three Cluniac houses in Scotland, Crossraguel is in the care of the State. Like many other Cluniac houses, it eventually rejected the dominance of Cluny, and became an abbey in its own right.

The Cluniac order came to place great emphasis on offering to God the best it could afford, with the result that its services became inordinately long and elaborate, and its buildings and their furnishings ever more opulent. But by the turn of the eleventh and twelfth centuries to many this began to seem at variance with the monastic vow of poverty, and a renewed movement for reform sprang up which resulted in the formation of several new orders of monks devoted to a simpler way of life. The most austere of these was the Carthusian order, founded by St Bruno at La Grande Chartreuse in southwestern France in 1084. But, since nothing survives of their one Scottish house, at Perth, no reference will be made below to this order, in which each house was essentially a community of hermits.

The Tironensian Order was founded by St Bernard of Tiron who, after various attempts to find a more satisfactory way of life, founded an abbey at Tiron, in northern France, in 1109. In his community the services were somewhat reduced in length to

12. The Cluniac abbey of Crossraguel, from the south. To the right are the walls of the fifteenth century choir, with its polygonal apse around the site of the altar. To the left, projecting at right angles, is the range which ran along the east side of the cloister, within which the chapter house and sacristy are particularly well preserved.

13. The Tironensian abbey of Kilwinning. The great gable of the south transept stands virtually complete, with its tall windows rising above the site of the adjacent east cloister range. To its left is one of the arches which opened into the chapels on the east side of the transept; projecting to its right is a fragment of the nave wall, which contains the processional door from the cloister.

14. Cistercian monks at work. This early twelfth century painting shows a monk chopping down a tree, with potentially dire consequences for the lay brother who is lopping its branches. (*Dijon, Bibliothèque Municipale, MS 173 f 41r*)

allow greater time for manual activity, and for contemplative exercise. Although Tiron never attracted a great following, it is an important indicator of David I's contact with the movement for monastic reform that the first foundation anywhere in Britain for a house of the reformed Benedictine orders was made by David, before becoming king, and that it was for the Tironensian order. This house, at Selkirk, was founded in 1113, but was later removed to Kelso, where it grew into a very prosperous abbey. The order eventually had eight houses in Scotland, three of which, at Arbroath, Kelso and Kilwinning, are in State care.

The Cistercian Order is the most famous of the reformed Benedictine orders. The mother house at Cîteaux, in Burgundy, was founded in 1098 by St Robert of Molesme, but the order owed its strength to two other remarkable individuals: St Stephen Harding, an Englishman, and another St Bernard. Stephen was the third abbot of Cîteaux, and before his death in 1134 he began to give the order the organisational basis which made its rapid growth possible. Bernard, who became abbot of Cîteaux's daughter house of Clairvaux, was one of the most influential writers of all times on the ideals of monasticism, and attracted vast numbers of recruits to the order.

Cistercian houses were founded away from centres of population, and under the influence of St Bernard there was early insistence that their buildings should be plain and without decoration. Although the monks were expected to undertake some manual work in the time left by the simplified services, they were also directed to spiritual activities, and to free them for this the heavy labour was undertaken by a lesser category of brothers known as the lay brethren. Since new Cistercian foundations were usually on previously uncultivated sites the initial labour involved might be massive, although it is an interesting reflection of the order's insistence on introverted self-sufficiency that they tended to be oustandingly efficient farmers.

The Cistercians were introduced into Scotland by David I at Melrose, in 1136, and eventually had twelve abbeys here, of which six are now in State care. These are at Melrose, Dundrennan, Glenluce, Culross, Deer and Sweetheart.

The Valliscaulian Order is one of the later and lesser known families of monasteries resulting from

the movement to reform. The rule of its mother house, at Val des Choux, in Burgundy, was given papal approval in 1205, and the order reached Scotland in 1230. Two of its three Scottish houses, at Ardchattan and Beauly, are in State care.

Although there was a growing tendency in the Middle Ages for monks to be ordained as priests, the founding fathers of monasticism had not envisaged priesthood as essential for monks. However, in parallel with the monastic movement, a number of communities of priests (known as regular canons because they followed a rule) were also founded, and these developed a form of life similar to that of the monks. The origins of this movement are uncertain, but in the eleventh century the same tendencies towards a stricter way of life which were affecting the monasteries also had an impact on the house of canons. In 1059 those canons who followed a way of life thought to be based on the teachings of St Augustine of Hippo, who had died in 430, came to be recognised as a distinct group known as Augustinian canons, and other groups of canons later emerged.

The Augustinian Canons attracted considerable patronage in Scotland, and eventually came to have

15. The church of the Valliscaulian priory of Beauly, which was founded in about 1230, viewed from the south-west. The church consisted of an aisle-less choir, from which transeptal chapels projected, and a similarly aisle-less nave. The western part of the latter was extensively remodelled by Prior Robert Reid after 1530. Evidence for the roofs of the cloister walks can be seen along the lower walls of the church.

16. The tower of the Augustinian abbey of Cambuskenneth. Founded by David I in about 1140, this abbey was amongst the richer houses of the order. The tower, which is mainly of later thirteenth century date, is the most complete surviving fragment of the abbey.

about eighteen houses. Their earliest Scottish house may have been Alexander I's foundation at Scone, of about 1120. The abbeys at Cambuskenneth, Inchcolm and Jedburgh are now in State care, along with the priories of Inchmahome, Loch Leven and Restenneth, and the great cathedral priory of St Andrews. In addition the State cares for the round tower of the early community at Abernethy which, like a number of other such communities, was for a time made into a house of Augustinian canons.

The Premonstratensian Canons were founded by St Norbert of Xanten at Prémontré, in north-eastern France, in 1120. St Norbert's aim was to introduce the same ascetic spirit into the life of the canons as had been formulated for the Cistercian order of monks, and the way of life of his canons showed many similarities with that of the Cistercians. The order was probably introduced into Scotland at Dryburgh, and of the six houses founded here the remains of two are in State care: Dryburgh Abbey, and the Cathedral Priory of Whithorn.

The Trinitarian Canons had about eight houses in Scotland. Of these the remains of only one, at Peebles, are in State care.

The periodic call to go back to a more essentially apostolic way of life, which had resulted in the great monastic reforms of the eleventh and twelfth centuries, in the thirteenth century led to the formation of the mendicant, or begging orders of friars. By the early thirteenth century it was becoming apparent that, even those orders of monks and canons founded with the purest intentions quickly became tramelled with worldly goods through the generosity of individuals attracted by that very purity. The founders of the two greatest orders of friars, St Francis and St Dominic, determined to renounce the world's goods more completely, and live on what they could beg. At the same time it was felt that it was not enough to follow the monks in turning away from the world and its snares, and it was decided that friars should live at centres of population, where they could preach to the people. Unfortunately, this preference for living in towns has meant that very few of their buildings have survived, and the only fragment now in State care is part of the Dominican church at St Andrews.

The Dominican Friars, or Friars Preachers (also known as Blackfriars from the colour of their habit) were instituted in 1215 by St Dominic at Toulouse, in south-western France, and took the rule attributed to

St Augustine as the basis of their life. St Dominic was strongly influenced by St Francis, whose order of friars received papal approval in the same year, but, whereas the unwordly St Francis had resisted efforts to regulate too precisely for his friars, the more practical St Dominic saw this as essential if his order were to flourish. The Dominicans reached Scotland in 1230, and the Franciscans (also known as Greyfriars) probably the year after. To fulfil their preaching role more effectively the mendicant orders developed close links with the universities, which were beginning to play a significant part in the intellectual life of Europe from the thirteenth century onwards. This may have been one reason why the Dominicans were attracted to St Andrews around the mid-fifteenth century, although it was only in the following century that their house there became an important one.

Brief reference must also be made here to the military orders, of which the remains of one house, at Torphichen, are in State care. The capture of Jerusalem in 1099 fired the imagination of Europe with a zeal for pilgrimage to the Holy Land, and created an awareness of the need for making access to the holy places safe. Orders of Knights living monastic lives were formed, with houses throughout

18. A friar at work in his study. The stress placed by the mendicant orders on both preaching and learning was clearly illustrated in the life of St Vincent, a Dominican friar, who is shown at his labours in this late fifteenth century painting. (*British Museum Royal 14E1 vol 1 f 3r*)

19. The transepts and tower of the church of the Knights Hospitaller at Torphichen. Although still incorporating work of the later twelfth century, the transepts were remodelled in the time of a fifteenth century preceptor of the house, Andrew Meldrum. The choir of the church has almost completely disappeared, but parts of the nave were absorbed into the post-Reformation parish church.

Europe, and David I introduced both the Knights Templars and Knights Hospitallers into Scotland.

The Knights Hospitallers, or Knights of the Hospital of St John of Jerusalem, were founded in the early twelfth century, at the height of the monastic reform movement, to care for the poor and sick and to provide escorts to the Holy Land. These Knights, who followed the rule of the Augustinian canons, eventually had three houses in Scotland, the earliest of which was that at Torphichen, which David I founded at some date between 1144 and his death in 1153.

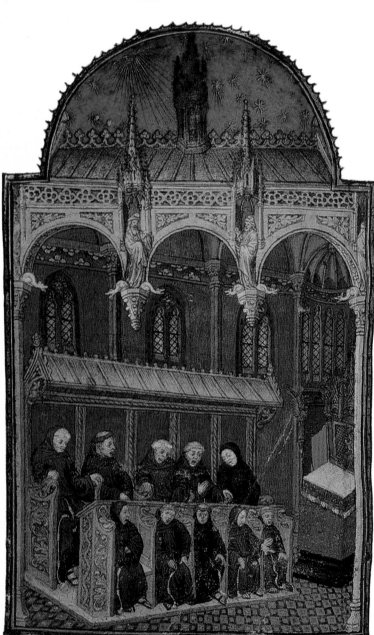

20. A depiction of a monastic choir at the time of a service. At the east end, within a polygonal apse, is the richly draped high altar, with an elaborate gilt reredos behind it, and curtains supported by riddel posts at the sides. The stalls run down the flanks of the choir, the floor of which is covered by what appear to be tiles. (*British Museum MS Cotton Dom A XVII f 122v*)

The Monastic Life

Although monastic life was to a considerable degree standardised, its form varied according to period, monastic order, and even time of year; the following is an outline of the daily life in the summer period of a monastery following the rule of St Benedict.

On a day which was not an important festival, the monks would rise about 1.30 in the morning and go down into the church for preliminary prayers followed by the first of their set services, Nocturns, which was sung at about 2.00. This, like the other services known as 'hours', consisted largely of psalms, prayers and readings. Matins followed at about 3.30 and after this there may have been a short rest before the daily washing of the face and hands; there may also have been some time for spiritual reading before a sequence of Prime at about 6.00 and the first mass of the day. After mass the community met in the main meeting room of the monastery, the chapter house, to read a chapter from St Benedict's rule, to discuss whatever was necessary and to confess misdemeanours. From about 7.30 there may have been a short period for work before Terce and Sung Mass followed at 8.00. Some two hours for reading started at around 9.30, after which came the service of Sext and then the main meal at about midday, which was followed by a rest period. The service called None probably started at about 2.30, after which was a period of work before supper at 5.30. Vespers began about 6.00, and then the monks changed into night shoes before going into the refectory at about 7.30 for a drink of some sort. The short service of Compline took place before the monks retired to the dormitory at about 8.15.

St Benedict had intended that all the monks, including their superior, should live, work and sleep as a community. But, as monastic life grew more complex, this became less feasible. Through the generosity of their founders and later patrons, the larger abbeys might become land-holding corporations of great wealth, the administration of which forced the head of the community (an abbot in an abbey, or a prior in a priory) to spend much of his time away from his monks. In larger houses the head tended to form a residence for himself apart from the main monastic complex from at least the twelfth century onwards. Additionally, since their responsibilities as feudal land holders, as monastic administrators, and as providers of hospitality meant they might have to feed important lay folk, their meals progressively became more lavish than the frugal vegetarian diet which the rule ordained for the monks.

The burdens of administration might also require the appointment of considerable numbers of officials, who themselves became increasingly separated from the life of the community. In an abbey the abbot would have one or more priors beneath him, whilst in a priory of any size there would be a sub-prior. In addition there might be a novice master over the new recruits, a precentor in charge of the abbey music, a sacrist responsible for the items used in church, a cellarer to organise the provisions of the community, an almoner who looked after the guests and an infirmarian to care for the sick and old monks in the infirmary. This by no means exhausts the list of officials, who may have numbered almost half the community in a large house.

The growing separation of officials and ordinary monks carried adverse consequences for monastic discipline. The officials were allowed certain privileges, which in turn led to general relaxations entering the life of many monasteries. For example, periodic culinary treats paid for by benefactors, and known as pittances, came to be allowed, whilst in some houses the monks might be allowed to eat occasionally at the table of the abbot or prior, or in the infirmary, where a more attractive diet could be served. At the same time the prohibition of unnecessary conversation became less complete, and locutoria (parlours or talking rooms) would be provided, or limited conversation might be allowed within the other buildings.

Monastic Planning

Planning of the main nucleus of monastic buildings tended to follow a set pattern. Although St Benedict appears not to have visualised any particular type of plan in formulating his rule, an early ninth century drawing for an ideal monastery, which has survived at the Swiss abbey of St Gall, shows that the form of plan which was to become so common was by then already known.

On a site where the fall of the land and the position of the water supply did not dictate otherwise, a monastery would usually be set out on the following lines. The church would be placed towards the north side of the site, with the main nucleus of monastic buildings around the other three sides of a rec-

21. The plan of Arbroath Abbey. The arrangement of the main nucleus of buildings around a square cloister illustrates the typical plan of a medieval monastery. However, the architectural requirements of an abbey as important as Arbroath were very diverse, and it can be seen that there were many other outlying buildings — although others have disappeared without trace.

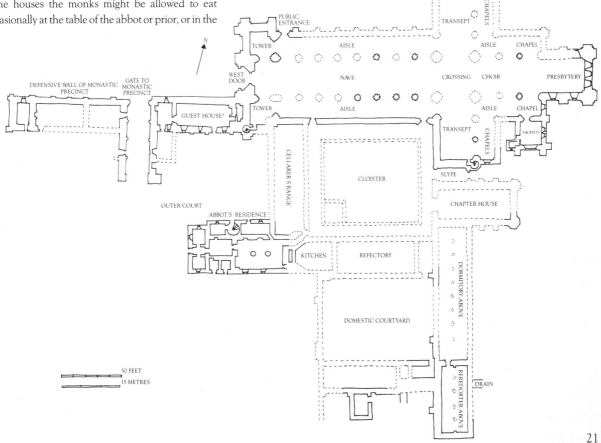

21

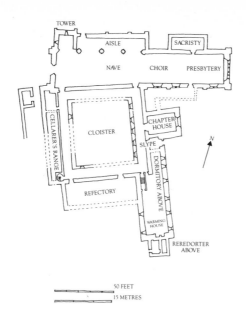

22. The plan of Inchmahome Priory. The basic arrangement of the buildings around an open cloister is similar to that of Arbroath. In such a smaller house, however, the plan is rather more compact, although a number of outlying buildings must certainly have disappeared.

Plan labels: TOWER · AISLE · SACRISTY · NAVE · CHOIR · PRESBYTERY · CELLARER'S RANGE · CLOISTER · CHAPTER HOUSE · SLYPE · DORMITORY ABOVE · REFECTORY · WARMING HOUSE · REREDORTER ABOVE · N

50 FEET
15 METRES

23. The refectory of Dunfermline Abbey. The majestic scale of the domestic buildings of an important abbey is here superbly illustrated. Possibly started in about 1329, the main dining hall had to be supported on two storeys of vaulted undercrofts because of the fall of the land. The pulpit, from which the monks heard appropriate readings whilst they ate, is indicated by the pair of narrow windows carried on an arch between two buttresses.

tangular area, known as the cloister, against the south flank of the church nave. On the east side of the cloister, and abutting the church transept if it had one, was a two-storeyed range, with the monks' dormitory on the upper level, and a variety of rooms at the lower. Two sets of stairs usually led down from the dormitory, one into the cloister for daytime use, and the other into the church for use at night. Amongst the lower rooms of the east range might be: the sacristy, where the priests prepared for services; a slype (passage) to the buildings on the east of the church and the monks' cemetery; the chapter house, which was the meeting place of the community; a locutorium, or parlour, where essential discussion was allowed; a calefactory or warming house, where the monks were permitted a fire to warm themselves. There might also be a room for the novices. At the end of this range would be the reredorter, or latrine, built over a drain supplied with running water. A particularly well-preserved example of an east range may be seen at Dryburgh Abbey.

The south range of the cloister was largely given over to the refectory, or eating hall, running either parallel or at ninety degrees to the church on the opposite side of the cloister. Some idea of the arrangement of a

refectory in a large abbey may be gained from the remains of that at Dunfermline; a more complete, but less typical example survives at Inchcolm. To the west of this hall, was usually the kitchen. The west range in most monasteries was the province of the cellarer, where he stored the provisions of the house, but in Cistercian abbeys it instead housed the lay brothers, who performed all the necessary labour of the community. As the heads of monasteries came to live more apart from their monks the first floor of the west range might sometimes also include a residence for the abbot or prior. In such a position it could still be seen as essentially a part of the communal buildings, whilst being conveniently close to the outer courtyard where the outside world came into closest contact with the monastery. At Arbroath a relatively modest first floor suite of rooms for the abbot was progressively enlarged to form a handsome semi-independent residence of such quality that it was retained for use as a house after the Reformation. (In Cistercian abbeys, however, the abbot's house might instead be placed to the east of the buildings around the cloister). The west range might also contain a second parlour where the monks could meet visitors under certain circumstances.

Around the perimeter of the open cloister were covered walkways which provided protected communication between the main buildings, and also afforded space for sedentary activities. In most cases these covered walks were lean-to structures, but occasionally, as at Inchcolm and Inchmahome, some of the walks might be incorporated in the lower level of the ranges around the cloister. In this they show similarities with a number of houses of friars in England, the urban settings of which placed space at a premium, and it may be that the island settings of these two houses also imposed economies of space.

Outside the main complex were many other buildings. Amongst these were the infirmary, which was usually to the south-east of the church, where the sick and aged monks were cared for in less strict circumstances than those which prevailed elsewhere in the monastery. There may also have been an adjacent misericord, where the other monks were on occasion allowed to take food forbidden in the refectory. Around the outer court of the monastery, which was usually placed to the west of the main buildings, between them and the outside world, were buildings to house the various functions requiring external contact. These included guest houses, barns, granaries, stables, bake-houses and brew-houses.

24. The abbot's house at Arbroath Abbey. Developed around a hall and bed-chamber at the junction of the south and west cloister ranges, the abbot's residence eventually grew to form a most imposing residence by the first half of the sixteenth century. The main entrance was through a (now blocked) door at first floor level, to the left of the group of three large windows, and would have been reached by an external flight of stairs.

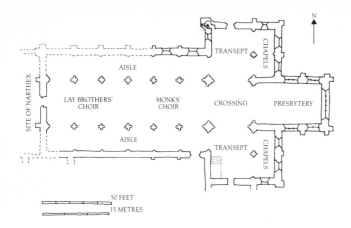

The plan diagram labels: SITE OF NARTHEX, AISLE, LAY BROTHERS' CHOIR, MONKS' CHOIR, CROSSING, PRESBYTERY, TRANSEPT, CHAPELS, TRANSEPT, CHAPELS, AISLE, N, 50 FEET, 15 METRES

25. The plan of Sweetheart Abbey. Despite being the last foundation for the Cistercian order in Scotland (it was founded in 1273), Sweetheart still conforms to the simple plan which had been adopted for the churches of the order in twelfth century Burgundy.

Amongst all of these buildings the church naturally had pride of place, and was usually the most architecturally distinguished structure. Despite differences of function, the abbey churches showed similarity of planning to the cathedral churches, except that the area occupied by the monks' choir stalls might extend down into part of the space which would be allotted to the lay folk in a cathedral. One major exception to this similarity, however, is the group of churches constructed for the Cistercian order, which forbade lay entrance to its churches. For this order a simple plan originally devised for its churches around the birth-place of the movement, in Burgundy, was at first used almost universally, and remained the norm for Scottish churches of the order. A plain rectangular presbytery for the high altar was flanked by transepts with chapels along their eastern side; to the west of this stretched the part of the building which would be used elsewhere as the nave, but which in Cistercian churches was divided into two separate choirs, one for the monks, and the other for the lay brothers. The early Cistercian churches were also forbidden the use of towers for their churches, although this ruling was disregarded in the later Middle Ages.

The Parish Churches and Chapels

The Emergence of a System of Parishes

Before the twelfth century it seems that the religious needs of the lay folk of Scotland had been rather patchily met by a variety of types of churches. In southern Scotland, and to a lesser extent elsewhere, it is likely that some of these churches were similar to the 'minsters' of pre-Conquest England: churches serving a large and sometimes undefined area, to which a group of priests was attached. It is also likely that a proportion of these churches had been first founded as monasteries but that the monks had progressively been replaced by communities of Culdees or other secular priests.

The more systematic provision of churches, each serving a specific area known as a parish, was a gradual process which took place mainly in the later eleventh and earlier twelfth centuries. Members of the royal family, bishops and other landholders came to see it as their duty to erect churches on their estates in order to provide for the spiritual welfare of themselves and their dependents. These churches would be endowed with enough land to support a priest, who was known as a rector or parson. This process was accelerated when the settlement of immigrant Anglo-Norman land-holders was fostered by successive kings, who were endeavouring to establish a system of feudal land-holding in their kingdom. It seems that grants of lands to these incomers may often have been conditional on the foundation and endowment of a church, especially during the reign of David I, who was particularly active in this process. To ensure that the parish priests were adequately supported David also encouraged the payment of teinds, (a tenth of the land's produce) to them, and this was later supported by an ecclesiastical council in 1177.

The network of parishes was virtually complete by the late thirteenth century, although there were never more than eleven hundred throughout Scotland, the vast majority being in the more settled areas of the south and east. However, these were partly supplemented by considerable numbers of chapels, particularly in the west, as well as by the later private chapels of landowners which were never drawn into the parochial network because of the resistance of the parish clergy to the subdivision of teinds. The remains of over thirty parochial churches or chapels are preserved in the care of the State.

24

The Appropriation of Parish Churches

Left to itself this network might have been modestly adequate for the Lowland areas at least, but the relative wealth of the parish churches was soon to prove an irresistible attraction to the cathedrals and monasteries. The patronage of a parish, that is the right to select who should be its rector, was generally regarded as belonging to the family which had founded the parish and its church, or their successors. It came to be considered an act of piety to give this patronage to a cathedral, monastery or other religious institution, but very often the body to which the patronage was given saw the endowment of these parishes as a means of making up its own financial deficiencies. In the great majority of cases these bodies arranged for the parishes over which they enjoyed patronage to be appropriated to them; that is, they assumed the great bulk of their income, thus becoming nominal rectors themselves. In their place they appointed a substitute, known as a vicar, to look after their parishioners, although where the appropriating body was a house of regular canons they might on occasion depute some of their own number to undertake the work of the parishes. Finally over eighty-five per cent of Scottish parishes were appropriated to some other religious body and, in addition, over half of these parishes eventually also had the income of their vicars appropriated, leaving barely sufficient subsistence for a curate.

Inevitably the parochial system became the poorest element in the Scottish Church, and the implications of this were of considerable negative significance. Many of the parish clergy appear to have been ill-educated and consequently unable to convey to their parishioners the Church's teachings, whilst the absentee rectors very frequently showed little concern for the structure of the choirs at their churches, for which the recipient of the teinds was responsible. The later Middle Ages showed some reversal of this situation, however, with the emergence of a greater emphasis on personal experience of religion, and a growth in the burghs of a sense of civic pride, of which the parish church was often a prime focus.

The Foundation of Chantries and Colleges

The Church in the late Middle Ages was in general both more conservative and introspective than it had been previously, whilst some of its institutions — perhaps most notably monasticism — were felt to be

26. A door from the church of Edrom. This fine doorway, which has been rebuilt as the entrance to a burial aisle, is characteristic of high quality earlier twelfth century work. The two orders of the arch have chevron (zig-zag) decoration, whilst the embracing hood mould has an embattled pattern; the vertical jambs have nook shafts set into the angles. The church may have been built by the cathedral priory of Durham, to which it was granted by Gospatrick, Earl of Dunbar, who died in 1138.

no longer fully meeting the needs for which they had developed. The uncertainties of the times, along with an increasingly inward-looking spiritual emphasis, fostered an almost morbid awareness of the sinfulness of humanity and the urgent need to make expiation for this sin if there were to be any hope of salvation. Religion consequently became a more personal matter, in which each individual had to be concerned to take steps to divert the threat of damnation.

Disillusionment first with the monastic, and later with the mendicant ideals, encouraged the laity to turn to the secular Church, and in particular to their parish churches. One of the most significant indicators of the religious climate of the times was a greatly increased provision for soul masses within parish churches and chapels. The Church had always taught that its prayers could obtain forgiveness for those who requested them in penitence, and so individuals would leave money in their wills to pay for masses to be said on behalf of their souls. But such bequests greatly increased in both numbers and scale in the later Middle Ages. Individuals, or groups such as craft guilds, who could afford to do so, might estabish a chantry for themselves: that is, they would leave sufficient funds for a succession of priests to

27. A requiem mass in a collegiate church. A prime function of such churches was the offering of prayers for the souls of their founders, and in this view the service which followed the founder's death is depicted. The draped coffin is enclosed within a frame-like hearse, which is covered by candles symbolising the upward ascent of the offered prayers. The coffin is placed in the main body of the choir, to either side of which are the stalls of the canons, whilst the altar and its reredos are covered by the same cloth as is used for the coffin pall. *(Paris, Musée Jacquemart-André MS 2 f 142v)*

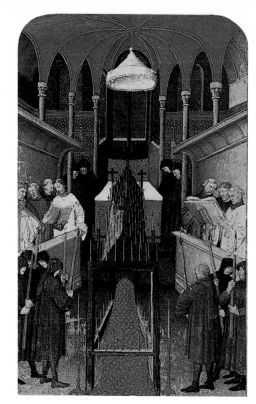

28. The collegiate church of Castle Semple, viewed from the north-east. A college was founded here in 1504 by Lord Semple, and the present church was presumably built about the same time. It is noteworthy for the rather curious design of the windows which pierce the walls of the polygonal apse around the site of the altar.

recite masses for the salvation of their souls in perpetuity. They might also provide an additional altar within their parish church, or even build a special chapel onto their church for this purpose. Some of the very wealthy — whose ancestors had founded many of the abbeys — went yet further, and founded colleges of priests within their local churches to pray for the salvation of their souls for all time coming.

Colleges of priests had a long history. The early communities of Culdees might be seen as representing a type of college, and at St Andrews around 1250 the successors of the Culdees who had previously served the cathedral church were formally made into a college, within the church of St Mary on the Rock. The chapters of canons who served cathedral churches might also be regarded as forming collegiate bodies. But the later medieval colleges were an expression of a rather different intention. A good example of such a college is that at Seton (figs 80 and 81), where successive Lords Seton rebuilt the choir of the parish church adjacent to their castle to accommodate the community of priests they had brought together to pray for their salvation, and for which they ultimately obtained the necessary papal approval to form a college in 1492. The remains of eight collegiate

churches are maintained by the State. In addition to those at St Mary on the Rock at St Andrews and Seton they are at Castle Semple, Dunglass, Innerpeffray, Lincluden, Maybole and Restalrig.

Sometimes the founder of a college would make additional provision for charitable functions, as at Lincluden (fig 74), where a number of old people were to be maintained within a hospital at nearby Holywood. But, when the founder was a prelate of the Church, he might choose rather to make these additional functions academic, since education was still chiefly in the hands of the Church. At St Andrews, for example, when Bishop Kennedy founded his college of St Salvator in 1450, he made provision for the maintenance of a number of masters and students at the university. Some of these colleges still fulfil part of the academic functions for which they were founded and, indeed, it is such bodies and their successors which are now most commonly associated with the notion of a college.

A related type of college was founded in the parish churches of several of the great burghs (although, since most of these happily remain in use, they are outside the scope of this book). Through the foundation of numbers of chantries these churches eventually came to have a considerable body of priests attached to them, and in several cases it was decided by the burgesses that the priests should be brought together in a collegiate body. By this means a seemly observation of the services and rituals was obtained, which could be seen as a fitting reflection of the corporate dignity of the burgh.

The Planning of Parish Churches and Chapels

Although the roles fulfilled by a parish church or chapel were less complex than those of a cathedral church, there was still the twin requirement of a space for the main altar and clergy, and an area for the lay folk. In the twelfth century this twin requirement was usually clearly expressed in the plan by the provision of a rectangular space for the choir to the east, and a larger rectangular space for the nave to the west. On occasions, following English examples, this plan might be further elaborated by providing an apse (curved extrusion) for the altar at the east end, and a square tower at the west end. The best preserved example of such a plan is at Dalmeny in West Lothian, but a less complete example may be seen in the church on the Brough of Birsay in Orkney.

After the twelfth century, church plans tended to become less ambitious: a considerable majority of Scottish churches was of unaugmented rectangular plan, with no structural distinction between choir and nave. There is some evidence that, in the later Middle Ages at least, some of these simple vessels might contain fine furnishings, and the separation of choir and nave would certainly have been clearly defined internally by a timber screen if not by the structure itself. But the widespread use of such a plan may be taken as an indicator of the poverty of much of the parochial network.

Two major exceptions to such simple planning were those churches in which a great landholder took an interest (particularly if they were family burial places), and the churches in the prosperous burghs. At the church of Douglas in Lanarkshire, the burial place of the Douglas family, we find the remains of an aisled nave, and an architecturally distinct aisle-less choir with a magnificent array of family tombs. The architecture may be even more elaborate at some of those churches which were erected into colleges. Seton and Dunglass, for example, not only have separated choir and nave, but flanking transepts to house additional altars. Seton, like several others, also has a polygonal apse at the east end to give prominence to the high altar, an indication of Scotland's inclination to look to the continent for some of its architectural inspiration in the later Middle Ages. The most unusual planning of any such rural collegiate church is at Rosslyn, where the choir follows the plan of Glasgow Cathedral in having aisles extending around three sides, and an eastern rank of chapels. But in general the largest and most complex churches were those of the wealthier burghs, where we commonly find not only aisles flanking the choir and nave, but additional chantry chapels tacked onto their sides, as at Holy Rude Church in Stirling.

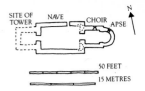

29. The plan of the church on the Brough of Birsay. Although diminutive in scale, this church shows the articulation of parts which might be found in the more ambitious Romanesque parish churches. A number of uses and dates of construction have been suggested for this church, although such a relatively sophisticated plan is unlikely to have been laid out before the earlier twelfth century.

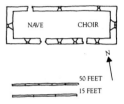

30. The plan of the late thirteenth century Kilbrannan Chapel at Skipness. This shows the simple rectangular planning which became characteristic of the majority of Scottish parish churches after the twelfth century; the distinction between the two principal parts of the building was not expressed in its plan.

31. The plan of Seton Collegiate Church. This cross-shaped plan was the result of several building campaigns. The fragmentary nave may be thirteenth century or earlier; the rest was built after the Seton family decided to found a college. The choir, with its polygonal eastern apse was built first, by the Lord Seton who died in about 1478. His great-grandson's widow added the transepts and tower in two operations in the central decades of the sixteenth century.

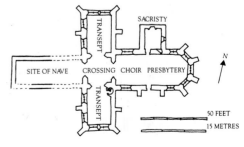

THE BUILDINGS

The Earliest Remains

UP TO THE 11TH CENTURY

The artistic resources of the early Church within what is now Scotland — an area of great political and cultural diversity before the twelfth century — are best illustrated by its carved remains. The stone cross at Ruthwell in Dumfriesshire, for example, shows how the traditions of the Mediterranean, rooted in the classical past, were able to reach that area — which was then a part of Northumbria — around the seventh or eighth centuries. Conversely, in those areas dependent on Ireland, high crosses of the eighth century, like that at Kildalton on Islay, show a preference for linear pattern-making inherited from the pagan North. Elsewhere in Scotland, throughout the area of the Pictish kingdom, cross slabs such as that in the Perthshire churchyard of Aberlemno also show developments on pre-Christian pattern-making, but combined with an anecdotal depiction of human activities.

The quality of such works is often outstandingly high, but it finds little reflection in surviving contemporary buildings; those early ecclesiastical remains which can still be identified are chiefly notable for their simplicity. Early monastic complexes, like those of Ireland, consisted of scatterings of crude huts around an equally unambitious oratory, and with a defensive rampart either encircling the site or cutting across the approach to it. A degree of skill is shown in the circular stone roofs of the twin cells on the island of Eileach-an-Naoimh in the Garvellachs, where a community may have been founded by St Brendan before his death in 577, and in which there is a debt to Irish prototypes of the sixth century. But there are few signs of any striving after architectural effects in Scotland before the eleventh century, even though the adjacent areas had already seen the emergence of a more monumental approach to design before then.

Nevertheless, some degree of awareness of architectural developments elsewhere is indicated by the

request of Nechtan, High King of the Picts, to Abbot Ceolfrid of Wearmouth for masons to build a church in 710. It may be that the earliest work at Restenneth Priory could be associated with that request, although the details of the masonry, and in particular the raised strip around its southern doorway, on balance appear more likely to date from the eleventh century. A similar doorway may be seen at the round tower of Abernethy, in Perthshire, which is one of only two such towers in Scotland. These towers represent a further import of Irish ideas, and illustrate the continuing influence of the Irish Church across much of Scotland before the twelfth century. The tower at Abernethy was probably raised around the end of the eleventh century, for the community of Culdee priests which was there at that time, although from changes in the character of the masonry it appears that the building had been started earlier and left incomplete. The other Scottish round tower is at Brechin, in Angus, where it was later absorbed into the medieval cathedral. A similar date as for Abernethy is indicated by the slender elegance of the figures which flank the entrance doorway, and which may be compared with figures on some of the later Irish high crosses.

One other eleventh century church about which it would be valuable to know more is that built by St Margaret at Dunfermline around the 1070's, and to which Archbishop Lanfranc of Canterbury sent Benedictine monks. Excavations have traced a simple two-part church, which was subsequently extended, below the nave of the abbey church. These foundations tell us little of the architectural character of the building, but the broader walls of its western part suggest it had a tower. It is tempting to make comparisons with the fascinating tower and church of St Rule at St Andrews, which had a plan of similar scale and proportions in its original form.

The date of St Rule's church, which was built for Scotland's premier bishop, is a perplexing problem. It is a possibility that the building is basically of the later eleventh century, although with major altera-

32. The round tower at Abernethy. The stripwork band of the doorway, and the form of the belfry windows suggest a date no earlier than the late eleventh century for this Irish-inspired tower, although there appears to be earlier masonry at the base of the tower. Originally it would probably have been capped by a pointed stone roof.

33. The tower and choir of the church of St Rule at St Andrews. The small scale and lofty proportions of this church, along with a number of its details, suggest it may have been built in the late eleventh century. The tall arch in the east wall of the choir (and a similar one in the west wall of the tower) were probably opened when the church was extended to house a community of Augustinian canons in the second quarter of the twelfth century.

tions made around the time that plans for installing a community of Augustinian Canons were under consideration by Bishop Robert between 1124 and 1144. From at least the tenth century St Andrews was regarded as the spiritual heart of the Scottish Church, and it would presumably have been provided with a church of architectural importance as soon as practically possible. The contacts which St Margaret established with the Anglo-Norman Church from about 1070 may have opened a channel for architectural ideas, and certainly a number of the details of St Rule's church suggest a knowledge of ideas current in England at the time that Saxon architectural traditions had not been entirely supplanted by those of the Normans. In particular, the construction of windows with both internal and external splays, and with arches cut into single blocks or through more than one masonry course, show techniques which were generally superseded in major buildings after the eleventh century. The same is true of the compressed plan and very lofty proportions. Any later date may seem additionally unlikely since it will be seen that, by the second quarter of the twelfth century, important buildings in Scotland were being erected to designs based on more recent English architectural ideas.

Anglo-Scottish Romanesque

THE EARLIER 12TH CENTURY

From what has been said it will be apparent that there is little evidence of any indigenous tradition of ecclesiastical architecture within what is now Scotland before the twelfth century; when the need for church buildings had arisen masons had probably been summoned from either Ireland or England to design them. It is therefore hardly surprising that, when the reorganisation of the Church in the earlier twelfth century created a need for new buildings on a hitherto unprecedented scale, there was an even greater demand for craftsmen. Although a much later account stated that David I called masons from the continent to work on one of his buildings, the archi-

tectural evidence of the twelfth century does not support this. Rather, the surviving buildings suggest that it was to Norman England that he and his supporters looked for architectural guidance, just as it was to England that they looked for guidance in determining how the Scottish Church should be organised. The Church in England was, of course, part of the Universal Church, and had enjoyed close links with Europe since William the Conqueror's efforts to bring it into line with the more advanced areas of the continent. Since 1066 English architecture had also come to play a significant role within the European context. Scottish ecclesiastical architecture was thus drawn into the mainstream of European ideas, but for some time to come it was essentially a part of a British current within that stream.

The range of architectural ideas taken up in Scotland is impressive, and the discernment shown in their choice indicates a wide awareness of Anglo-Norman architecture. This may suggest that David I, with his close knowledge of many parts of England, took a personal interest in the design of some of the churches which were beginning to rise across the more settled parts of his kingdom. At Dunfermline, for example, where David's additional gifts to the community founded by his mother encouraged the building of a new abbey church in about 1128, its design looks to the northern English cathedral of Durham. By the time of the death of Bishop Flambard of Durham in 1128 work on that cathedral was nearing completion, and it may be suspected that some of its masons were attracted to the works at Dunfermline.

The twelfth century choir, which would have been the first part of the church to be built, has gone and we cannot know how closely it was modelled on Durham; but certainly the eastern parts of the lowest stage of the nave show similarities, on a smaller scale, with Durham. Its heavy cylindrical piers decorated by incised ornament, with octagonal cushion capitals are very like alternate piers at Durham. Other parallels with Durham can be seen in the design of the aisles, which are covered by ribbed vaults and have decorative arcading below the single round-headed window in each bay. As was usual in greater churches by the twelfth century, the interior was divided horizontally into three distinct stages: an arcade of tall arches opening into the flanking aisles; a gallery, or triforium, at the level of the roofs over the aisles; a clerestory to light the central part of the building, with windows set back on the outer face of a mural

34. The nave of Dunfermline Abbey church. A church was built here in about 1070, but the present building was probably started around 1128 when the foundation was splendidly re-established for a community of Benedictine monks. The debt to Durham in the design of the arcade piers is evident; the more elaborate pier in the foreground of this view dates from repairs made in the time of Abbot Richard de Bothwell (1446-82).

passage. However the upper stages of the nave were built to a much plainer design than those of Durham, suggesting that guidance from that source was no longer available by the time the gallery and clerestory were under construction. In each bay the upper stages have only one round-headed opening, the severity of which is partly relieved by a single shaft on each flank.

In the same year that work probably started at Dunfermline, the Tironensian community at Selkirk was transferred to a more suitable site at Kelso, and work on an abbey church there was commenced soon afterwards. Kelso is a difficult building to understand both because it is incomplete and because it seems to have taken a very long time to build, with consequent changes in design in the course of the work. Although its east end was sufficiently complete for David I's son,

Henry, to be buried there in 1152, the upper parts of the west end were under construction for many years. Its plan was in the form of a double cross, with transepts at both ends; similar plans had earlier been common around the Rhine valley, and were also to be found in the East Anglian abbeys of Bury St Edmunds, Ely and Peterborough. Yet the interior of Kelso appears to have shown few debts to those areas. The three stages of the internal elevation were designed as continuous lines of round-headed arches, and one of the few other buildings which shows a similar arrangement is the collegiate church of St John in Chester. At both these churches construction of the nave seems to have been unusual in that it proceeded layer by layer from bottom to top, rather than in bays from east to west, and in both cases the upper levels are much later than the lower. But Kelso is

35. The nave of Kelso Abbey. Although probably started soon after its transference to Kelso from Selkirk in 1128, the surviving fragment of the nave of this Tironensian abbey church shows that building took many years to complete. The arcade, which was completed first, is remarkable for its heavy strength, but a greater sense of structural lightness can be seen entering the moulded details of the upper storeys.

36. The western bays of the choir of Jedburgh Abbey. Founded for Augustinian canons in about 1138, the choir was probably the first part of the abbey church to be completed. Its unusual design, in which the intermediate stage appears to be slotted into the arcade arches, is based on a small number of southern English churches, of which Romsey is perhaps the immediate source. The clerestory and eastward extension of the choir were part of a modification which took place around the turn of the twelfth and thirteenth centuries.

All of these churches were planned on a lavish scale which was unprecedented in Scotland, and which must have made clear that a major change was taking place within the Scottish Church. But the decoration which was applied to them could equally well be applied to smaller churches. The chevron (zig-zag) ornament found in the arches around the door heads at Dunfermline abbey — which are characteristically stepped outwards in a series of distinct orders — or in the gallery arches at Jedburgh, is repeated around the chancel arch of the small castle chapel of St Margaret at Edinburgh. This much-altered structure was probably built for David I around the 1120s. Similar chevron decoration is also found as far apart as a doorway of the Berwickshire parish church at Edrom (fig 26), which may have been built around the time it was given to Durham cathedral by the Earl of Dunbar between 1128 and 1138, as well as on the chancel arch of the church of St Blane on Bute, for which no certain date is known.

It was in the design of their decorative capitals, however, that the individual masons were allowed to show their greatest ingenuity, although the loss of their painted colouring means that we no longer see these capitals as their masons intended. The most rudimentary type of capital was that of cushion form, as seen in several varieties at Dunfermline. The scallops of the caps at Kelso are one stage removed from this basic form, although the sculptors of the twelfth century had many other ways of introducing variety into their work. A first step in the emergence of decorative relief is seen in the west door of Dunfermline, where the semi-circular surfaces of both cushion and scallop caps are slightly cut back, but far greater richness of treatment is seen in the door at Dunfermline which acted as the processional entrance from the cloister. Some of the caps of this door still show the residual outline of cushion or scallop shapes by means of curved bands, but the surfaces have been deeply excavated to create lush patterns of formalised foliage, sometimes with grotesque animal heads at the angles, where the design might otherwise have been weakest. As might be expected at Dunfermline, these carved capitals show similarities to work at Durham, and in particular to some displaced fragments from the old chapter house of about 1140.

At Dunfermline the residual outline of the cushion or scallop shapes ensures a satisfying coherence to several of the carved capitals, and this is also seen on some of the caps of Edrom, which may equally have

additionally unusual because there appears to have been no attempt to divide the triforium and clerestory levels into vertical bays corresponding to the arcade piers. As at Dunfermline, the piers of Kelso are of massively cylindrical shape, although they are more squat and additional elements project from them to support parts of the arcade arches and the aisle vaults; their scalloped caps are a variant on the cushion caps seen for example at Dunfermline.

In the abbey for Augustinian Canons, which David I and Bishop John of Glasgow founded at Jedburgh in about 1138, further evidence of a wide search for architectural ideas is to be seen. Here the earliest parts of the choir were built so that the intermediate gallery stage appears to be suspended within the arcade, which is itself carried on cylindrical piers of very tall proportions. Related designs are found in a small number of churches in western and southern England, of which the nunnery church at Romsey, in Hampshire, shows the closest parallels to Jedburgh. Significantly, David I's aunt Christina was a nun at Romsey, whilst his sister Matilda had stayed there before becoming the queen of Henry I, and the choice of Romsey as an architectural inspiration is thus perhaps hardly surprising.

37. The interior of the chapel of St Margaret in Edinburgh Castle. The decoration of the arch at the entrance to the semi-circular apse suggests a date around the 1120s for the construction of this small building. Although the barrel vault which covers the nave appears in keeping with the rest of the building, it was only constructed when the chapel was converted into a powder magazine.

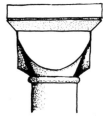

38. A cushion capital. A principal function of the cap in Romanesque architecture was to effect the transition between the round section of the supporting shaft, and the square section of the supported arch. One of the simplest ways of doing this was by means of the block-like cushion cap, the design of which was imported to Britain from the area of the Rhine valley. Its plain faces must often have been covered with painted decoration.

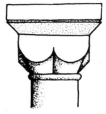

39. A scallop capital. Caps of this sort were a rather more decorative derivative of the cushion form.

40. The carved capitals of the processional entrance doorway into Dunfermline Abbey church from the cloister. The lush foliage with which these caps are decorated is closely related to designs in contemporary manuscript painting, from which the sculptors probably took their ideas. Even the flat abacus, which separates each cap from its arch, is here elaborately carved, and when the detail was picked out in colour the effect must have been extremely rich.

41. A volute capital. Such designs, which had been popular in Normandy before the Conquest of England, represent one of the oldest types of Romanesque capital. The curved volutes at the angles, along with the stylised leaf forms, are clearly based on the Corinthian capitals of Greece and Rome — a reminder that the remains of classical antiquity continued to exert an influence throughout the Middle Ages.

42. A capital at St Bride's Church, Douglas. Although badly mutiliated, this fine example of a later twelfth century cap illustrates how closely based on classical prototypes such caps might be.

43. The church of St Magnus, on the Orkney island of Egilsay. This church was built on the site where Earl Hakon had murdered his cousin, Earl Magnus, at Easter in 1116. It is difficult to date such churches on the architectural evidence, although the central decades of the twelfth century appear most likely. The design of the church appears to owe much to Irish prototypes.

been the work of Durham masons. But in some other cases the foliage spreads across the capital in a more freely decorative manner, which is perhaps reminiscent of contemporary English metalwork and ivory carving, and which provides a valuable illustration of how one art form might influence another. Another commonly found type of capital in twelfth century Scotland, which is also to be seen in the west door of Dunfermline, is the volute cap, a form ultimately derived from the Corinthian capitals of classical antiquity. Amongst the variants of this type must be included a displaced example in the Lanarkshire church of St Bride at Douglas.

Although the buildings so far discussed are concentrated chiefly in the Lowlands, where royal control and influence were most complete, the architectural changes were not to be confined to those areas. One other area which saw the construction of new churches was Orkney. In the twelfth century the Northern Isles were still Norse, but parallels with Lowland Scotland are to be seen in the importation of Anglo-Norman masons for the construction of the new cathedral at Kirkwall after Earl Rognvald had removed the see there in 1137. Elsewhere in Orkney, the twelfth century witnessed the construction of a

number of churches which are remarkable for the variety of their planning. At Wyre the shell of the church is a simple two-part structure, but at Egilsay a tall round western tower and vaulted substructure to the choir give an unusual interest to the church raised where St Magnus had been murdered in 1116. At Orphir the circular shape of the nave may be a consequence of Earl Hakon's visit to the shrines of the Holy Land to obtain forgiveness for the murder of St Magnus. It is also a possibility that the plan of the church on the Brough of Birsay belongs to this phase of architectural innovation, rather than to any earlier period (fig 29).

The advantages of a revitalised church eventually became apparent to the semi-autonomous rulers of the Western Highlands and Islands, as may be seen in the area controlled by the Lords of the Isles. On Iona, Reginald, son of Somerled, refounded an abbey shortly before 1203 on the venerable site of Columba's community, and probably also established the nearby nunnery for Augustinian canonesses shortly afterwards. Chronologically these two buildings should more correctly be referred to in a later part of this book, except that the architecture of their earliest buildings is still fully Romanesque in character. The reason for this is not simple architectural conservatism, but the likelihood that Reginald's masons were drawn from Ireland, where Romanesque forms remained in vogue after being superseded elsewhere in the British isles. This illustrates that, for the West, water-borne contact with Ireland was often easier than contact across land routes with the Lowlands.

The Transition from Romanesque to Gothic

MID TO LATER 12TH CENTURY

The movement away from the heavy, robust strength of Romanesque architecture towards the lighter, more attenuated refinement of Gothic, along with the more general structural use of pointed rather than round arches, was well under way within the Royal Domain of France during the second quarter of the twelfth century. Some decades later the impact of these ideas began to be felt in English architecture, and from there the ideas spread north of the border. Scotland could seldom afford buildings employing the full Gothic structural system, in which high vaults supported by a complicated framing of buttresses created an impression of weightless stone. Nor were

the more elaborate Gothic eastern terminations, with ranks of chapels around a tall polygonal apse, ever attempted here. Nevertheless, during the third quarter of the twelfth century a new spirit can be discerned to be entering into Scotland's major buildings which, by the end of the century, had taken concrete form in a manner of design which is clearly Gothic — even if its summits of achievement are more modest than those of England or France.

An appropriate climate for Lowland Scotland to receive these ideas was created by its strong architectural contacts with northern England. That area had been widely settled by monks of the Cistercian Order, whose buildings included much that was imported from France. In their earlier churches the ideas were drawn from the order's

44. The east gable of St Andrews Cathedral. This was probably the first part of the cathedral, started in about 1160, to rise to a significant height. Originally it was pierced by three ranks of three round-headed windows each; only the lowest tier survives, but the ghosts of the others can be seen around the edge of the large window inserted by Prior Haldenstone (1418-43).

45. The south transept of St Andrews Cathedral. The remains of the decorative intersecting arcading run along the base of the wall, although the free-standing shafts which connected caps and bases have gone. Similar arcades used to run along the lower walls of the presbytery, but all except the bases (which were covered by a raised floor) were swept away in the fifteenth century re-arrangement of the choir and presbytery.

46. A chalice capital. Like the earlier cushion cap, the chalice cap was a very simple means of making the transition from shaft to arch. Its extreme plainness made it acceptable to the Cistercians, who were probably responsible for introducing it to Britain.

47. A water-leaf capital. The shape of a water-leaf cap is very like that of the chalice cap, and the two varieties are often found side-by-side in the same building. An appearance of broad and fleshy leaf forms, which usually curl up at the angles, is created by surprisingly little cutting into the body of the cap. After being made popular by the Cistercians, more elaborate variants on this idea were developed (see fig 49).

original home in Burgundy, although the Cistercians of Yorkshire later began to look to northern France as well. In their buildings we find the early use of pointed arches, within a severe architectural context which allowed the structural framework to be clearly expressed, and, although such architecture was not in itself Gothic in character, it created an environment within which Gothic could happily take root.

The most important building to be started in the mid-twelfth century was Scotland's premier cathedral, at St Andrews. The new cathedral was begun by Bishop Arnold, in or soon after 1160, and was set out on the vast scale introduced for several of the major English churches planned since the Norman Conquest. The choir was given arcades of five bays with a deeply projecting rectangular presbytery beyond (fig 7), whilst a nave of fourteen bays was laid out, but was later reduced to twelve. A greater contrast with the compressed scale of the earlier church of St Rule, which was retained to the south-east of the new building (fig 33), could hardly be imagined.

In much of its design, such as the elaborately decorative intersecting arcading of the lower walls, which still survives in the south transept, and in the tiers of round-arched windows which originally pierced its eastern wall, the building was still clearly Romanesque. But its details show a lighter spirit entering the work as building progressed, and it was eventually decided to construct a high vault over the choir. Much of this new spirit was inspired by northern England, and it is likely that the master mason in charge of the work came from that area. Although the building is

extensively ruined, it can be seen that the piers of the arcade consisted of bundles of eight shafts, the appearance of which would have been markedly more elegant than that of earlier types. Piers of this sort may have been first introduced into England from Burgundy at the Yorkshire Cistercian abbey of Kirkstall in the 1150s, and they were afterwards used widely in northern England. Further clues to the influence of that area on St Andrews may be detected in some of the decorative capitals. The earliest surviving caps are decorated with crockets (curled leaf forms) at the angles, but two other types were soon introduced which were particularly favoured by the Cistercians in both Burgundy and Northern England on account of their simplicity. These were the so-called chalice and water-leaf capitals.

A similar picture as at St Andrews of changing architectural ideas is seen in the continuing work at Kelso Abbey (fig 35), and it may be of significance that Bishop Arnold of St Andrews had earlier been Abbot of Kelso. In the triforium stage of Kelso, which is carried on round shafts, many of the capitals are of scalloped type, like those of the arcade below, although a number of water-leaf caps are interspersed amongst them. But at clerestory level there is a greater change. The arches are still round, yet the small piers which carry them are made up of triplets of shafts which, like the shafted piers at St Andrews, are more graceful than cylindrical piers, and their caps are chiefly of water-leaf and crocket type.

The building which now most clearly illustrates the transition from Romanesque to Gothic is the Cistercian abbey of Dundrennan in Kirkcudbrightshire. The abbey was probably founded in 1142, with monks from the north Yorkshire abbey of Rievaulx, and it is likely that the church was built soon afterwards to the simple plan type preferred by the Cistercians. The abbey prospered, and after about thirty or forty years the transepts underwent a major remodelling. The two chief sources of inspiration for the new work were the Yorkshire Cistercian houses at Roche and Byland. The former was probably built shortly before 1170, and the latter may have been started at about the same time, although the construction was to be a lengthy process. In all of these churches there is a modified attitude to the Cistercian requirement of austerity. It is respected in the simplicity of carved details, with caps chiefly of chalice or water-leaf form; yet the overall designs are less plain than might have been expected. This is particularly evident in that, instead of leaving the area between arcades and clerestory blank, as had been customary in earlier Cistercian churches, this area is instead decorated by bands of arches or is treated as a triforium.

Although the result of the remodelling at Dundrennan is extremely handsome, there are several incongruities in the way the new work is grafted onto an existing building. The tall pointed arches of the arcades contrast oddly with the squat round-arched clerestory windows, which were probably retained from the original structure, whilst changes at triforium level between the two transepts appear indecisive. Nevertheless, the refinement of the new arcades, with piers composed of bundled shafts topped by chalice caps, and with finely moulded arches, marked an important stage in the movement towards acceptance of Gothic in Scotland.

Other buildings show different aspects of current architectural ideas. At the Augustinian abbey of Holyrood, which had been founded by David I in 1128, construction of a larger nave was started to the north of the existing building in the last decades of the twelfth century. In its elaborate intersecting round arches the wall arcading which decorates this work could still be described as Romanesque, except that its mouldings show a new finesse. However, most of the wall arcade caps are elaborations on crocket and water-leaf forms, and some of the leaves which project at the angles of these caps are beginning to show similarities to the type of foliage which is known as stiff-leaf (see page 43).

48. The north transept of Dundrennan Abbey. The remodelling of the transepts in the last quarter of the twelfth century was probably undertaken by masons who had previously worked on northern English Cistercian buildings. The tall arcade, which opens into the eastern chapels, and the decorative band of blind arches at triforium level, show the attenuated proportions and finely moulded detailing of Early Gothic architecture.

49. A cap from the north aisle arcade of Holyrood Abbey. Although essentially of water-leaf form, the original simplicity of this type of cap has been abandoned in the first phase of reconstruction of Holyrood nave. Above the water-leaf forms is a second tier of foliage, some of which shows the three formalised leaves of the type known as 'stiff-leaf' (see fig 58).

50. Inchcolm Abbey from the east. Across the ruins of the late medieval choir and transepts may be seen the central tower of the earlier church (the cloister buildings and chapter house lie to the left). Within the large arch at its base are the three smaller arches which originally rose above the pulpitum at the west end of the canons' choir, but which has itself been breached by a later arch.

51. The south door of Auchindoir Church. The principal entrance to this otherwise rather unassuming rectangular church is emphasised by a finely decorated doorway. The combination of mouldings which continue unbroken around the opening with others supported by nook shafts (the shafts themselves have gone), is characteristic of work at the turn of the twelfth and thirteenth centuries.

Approximately contemporary with this work at Holyrood are the lower stages of the tower added to the Augustinian house on the island of Inchcolm, in the Firth of Forth. This tower is of special interest for incorporating a valuable illustration of the way in which the parts of an abbey church might be sub-divided. Within the arches at its base are the remains of the pulpitum and rood screen separating the monks' choir from the nave. Above screen walls, pierced by access doorways, the pulpitum was extended into an arcade of three arches, with two arches above the corresponding rood screen to its west. The arches were carried on water-leaf capitals displaying a similar elaboration as at Holyrood.

In looking at the abbeys and cathedrals it should not be forgotten that they were not the only churches under construction. It is perhaps true that one result of the appropriation of teinds was a diminution of parish church construction from the later twelfth century onwards. Nevertheless, even despite the post-Reformation loss of a high proportion of Scotland's medieval churches, there is still evidence of some continuing effort to provide fitting churches for those parishes where this had not already been achieved. A good illustration of this is the church of Auchindoir in Aberdeenshire. Like many churches built after the mid-twelfth century its plan is a simple rectangle, but its south doorway shows that the church was designed by a mason of some competence. The outer order of this round-headed opening is carried on shafts with handsome crocket caps, and there is a projecting hood mould which is decorated by dog-tooth mouldings (pyramidal shapes with hollowed flanks).

An architectural stage approximately parallel to that of Auchindoir is represented by the chapel adjacent to the MacDougall castle of Dunstaffnage in Argyll. Of similar rectangular plan, its architecture also shows an intermingling of round and pointed arches, and an even richer taste for bands of dog-tooth ornament. In this case the most prolific display of dog-tooth was concentrated in three pairs of fine windows around the site of the altar. However, it is likely that the Dunstaffnage chapel must be dated well into the first half of the thirteenth century since, as at the abbey and nunnery of Iona, the immediate architectural debt is to Ireland rather than England.

52. One of the pairs of windows which flank the site of the high altar at Dunstaffnage Chapel. In their combination of continuous and supported mouldings, and the use of dog tooth decoration, these windows show parallels with the door at Auchindoir. When the walls were plastered and painted, and the furnishings associated with the altar were in place, this chapel must have presented a splendid appearance.

53. The east end of the presbytery at Arbroath Abbey. The tiers of triplets of lancet windows in the projecting presbytery gable invite comparison with St Andrews, although the architecture clearly belongs to a later period.

Early Gothic

By the end of the twelfth century the major buildings under construction in Scotland may fairly be described as being Gothic in character. The architectural changes that had been effected by this period may be seen by comparing the earlier parts of the cathedral of St Andrews and the Tironensian abbey of Arbroath in Angus.

Arbroath had been founded in 1178 by King William the Lion to appease St Thomas Becket, whom the king believed to have been instrumental in his capture at the battle of Alnwick, although it is likely that the construction of its church was postponed for some years. The design of Arbroath shows many similarities with St Andrews, on a smaller scale, particularly in its plan (fig 21) and in the internal design of its presbytery and choir; the differences between the two are thus easily observed. The eastern wall of Arbroath, with its decorative arcading running around the base of the interior, and with triplets of windows at each stage of the elevation, is of a similar design to that of St Andrews (fig 44). But the relative mass of the wall has been reduced even further, whilst the arches of the arcades and windows are now pointed rather than round-headed; it should be added, however, that in the south transept some of the arches are still round-headed, showing that either arch form was still considered acceptable.

It would be of interest to know how far the design of Arbroath was dependent on that of St Andrews. A major building operation was doubtlessly always a stimulus to other buildings in its area and, in addition to the major similarities already mentioned, the two churches had many details in common, including the basic form of the arcade piers, for example. But the design of Arbroath also shows an infusion of new ideas which makes it justifiable to describe it as Gothic by comparison with the late Romanesque of the choir of St Andrews, and to see where these newer ideas came from we must look once more to northern England. The clearest evidence is for the design of the interior. On the evidence of the single surviving bay beneath the north-west tower, Arbroath's appearance was strikingly like that of the choir of the Augustinian priory of Hexham in Northumberland, which was started in about 1180. It thus seems likely that, although the mason who designed Arbroath knew the work at St Andrews, he was also acquainted with more recent work such as Hexham, and may even have worked there. Comparison of architectural and sculptural details supports this link, although for a structure as complex as Arbroath it is likely that its designing mason drew his ideas from a wide range of buildings. For the design of the west front, with its combination of twin towers and a large central round window, the master mason showed particular ingenuity; there is even a possibility that he may have been aware of current architectural ideas in France, where such a combination of forms was becoming common.

Another building being erected around the same time as Arbroath was the nave of Jedburgh Abbey which, apart from its aisle walls, survives in a

54. The north-west corner of the nave of Arbroath Abbey. The three stages of the internal elevations of the abbey church have been preserved at this point. At the base is an arch of the arcade which opened into the flanking aisle, and the gallery and clerestory rise above it.

55. The nave of Jedburgh Abbey. Jedburgh now gives the most complete impression of the internal appearance of a great Scottish abbey church of the Early Gothic period, and comparison with the interior of Dunfermline (fig 34) illustrates the remarkable changes in architectural design which had taken place over about half a century. At Dunfermline the impression is of masses of walling of great strength, but at Jedburgh the reduction of the areas of unbroken wall, along with the definition of each opening by elegantly linear mouldings, creates an air of effortless lightness.

56. An arcade capital at Jedburgh Abbey. The fleshy water-leaf foliage of this cap shows similarities with northern English work, as at the Cistercian abbey of Byland. A similar debt may be indicated by the pier and the arch mouldings, which are both of types favoured by the Cistercians.

57. The south side of the nave of Holyrood Abbey. Despite being badly damaged by the collapse of its high stone vault in 1768, the surviving fragments of Holyrood still display its superb quality. The south arcade and triforium survive virtually complete, but the clerestory, which was embraced by the vault, is gone.

remarkably complete state. Jedburgh and Arbroath have much in common. The piers of the arcades at both churches are composed of bundles of eight keeled (pointed) shafts, the gallery openings of both are of two pointed arches within a round-headed containing arch and, although the evidence of Arbroath is incomplete, it is possible that the clerestory was similar to that of Jedburgh in having two windows to each bay behind an arcaded wall passage. Nevertheless there are significant differences in their relative proportions, which suggest that the similarities may have been as much a consequence of their masons coming from the same area as of any more direct link between the two.

At Arbroath the red sandstone from which the abbey is built has decayed so badly that very little carved detailed has survived. Conversely, Jedburgh is particularly memorable for its architectural sculpture, and the arcade piers carry an unsually fine array of foliage caps, some of which invite comparison with those of the Yorkshire abbey of Byland. Many of these caps are of crocket form, whilst others are inventive developments on the water-leaf type, which leave the earlier Cistercian simplicity far behind.

The resumption of work to a modified design on the nave of Holyrood abbey, and its completion around the second decade of the thirteenth century, marked a high water mark of Early Gothic architecture. Unlike Arbroath and Jedburgh, Holyrood was designed to have a stone vault over the central part of the nave, as well as over the aisles, and it is clear that the whole project must have been financed on a lavish scale. Analogies for parts of its design may be seen in the choir of Lincoln cathedral, started in 1192, particularly in the design of the triforium and high vault. However, the masons of Holyrood did not follow the English masons in all aspects of their work. One of the ideas with which English masons were experimenting at this time was the reduction of arcade piers to as small a core as possible, with surrounding free-standing shafts in a contrasting colour. But at Holyrood concern for the support of the vault led to the design of more massive piers of stepped plan and with attached shafts in the angles, which are still of an essentially Romanesque type. It is perhaps an indicator that masons working in Scotland were beginning to develop a more independent attitude to architectural design, that variations on such piers were to remain standard for many of the major churches of the thirteenth century.

One of the delights of Holyrood is its foliage carving. Much of the thirteenth century foliage is of comparable standard to the earlier caps in the north aisle, although different in style. The later work, which is mainly of the type known as stiff-leaf, is best seen in the south aisle wall arcade, where the vault has protected it from the elements. Several sculptors were involved in the carving of these capitals, with consequent variations in the quality of the work, but in the best the carving shows the balance between spirited freedom and a sense of harmonious balance which is the mark of good architectural sculpture.

Similar foliage, albeit of lesser quality, is found in the chapter house at Inchcolm abbey, on the central boss at which the vaulting ribs converge. This structure was built in the early years of the thirteenth century, and is one of only three octagonal chapter houses known to have been built in Scotland (fig 50), the others being at Holyrood abbey (now destroyed) and Elgin Cathedral. Centralised chapter houses of either circular or polygonal form are known to have been built at about twenty-five churches in England, but rectangular structures were always more common. One of the most complete of these in Scotland is at Dryburgh Abbey, a house of Premonstratensian Canons in Berwickshire. The abbey was founded in 1150, and the range on the east side of the cloister which included the chapter house was built in the later decades of that century.

The choir of the church at Dryburgh appears to have been planned at the same time as the east range, but it is unlikely that work on it was seriously undertaken

58. A cap from the wall arcading in the south aisle of Holyrood Abbey. This apparently wind-swept foliage is of the type now known — rather inappropriately — as stiff-leaf. It is characterised by the three lobed leaves to each stem.

59. The north transept and choir of Dryburgh Abbey. This early thirteenth century Premonstratension abbey church relies on fine proportions and simplicity of detail for effect, an effect which is enhanced by its magnificent setting. The irregular coursing of the masonry around the openings at triforium level suggest these were later insertions.

before the early thirteenth century. Only part of the north side of the choir and the adjacent north transept survive in anything approaching completeness, and this fragment has itself undergone considerable repairs following fires caused by English troops in 1322 and 1385. It is nevertheless easy to see that, as befitted the church of an order committed to a life of austerity, it relied on fine proportions rather than elaboration of detail for its chief impact.

The plan of the choir was a compressed version of that at St Andrews and Arbroath, with chapels in the aisles flanking transept and choir. The arcades rise to about half the height of the internal elevations, and above this the walls are divided into vertical bays by shafts and into horizontal stages by string courses. At clerestory level the internal arcaded passage is

deepened below the windows, thus reducing the triforium stage to about half the height of the clerestory. Each bay of the triforium has a circular opening within an arched recess, but it is likely that these openings were only inserted after one of the fires, and that originally this stage was left as blank walling. (The Premonstratensian canons took many of their principles from the Cistercians, whose original rejection of galleries or triforia has already been mentioned.) Externally the walls of Dryburgh emerge from a deep moulded base course, and are divided into bays at aisle and clerestory level by broad buttresses. A continuous string course, on which the single-light aisle windows rest, steps up on the gable wall of the transept beneath the larger grouped windows in that wall. The sense of harmony and of logical relationship between the parts is characteristic of the finer buildings of its generation, and demonstrates that they are part of an architectural tradition which has already reached a high level of sophistication.

60. The crypt of Glasgow Cathedral. This view, looking towards the Lady Chapel and the eastern chapels beyond, shows the fascinating spatial complexity of this part of the cathedral.

Mature Gothic

MID TO LATER 13TH CENTURY

In the mid-thirteenth century the pace of new building continued unabated, but a higher proportion of effort was now being expended on the cathedrals than on the churches of the monks and canons. This was partly because many of the abbeys were already well provided with buildings, but also because the monastic ideal was no longer attracting such munificent patronage, and fewer monasteries were consequently being founded.

Of several major campaigns instigated in the central decades of the thirteenth century, one of the most important was the choir of Glasgow (fig 9). The diocese had been re-established by David I at some date between 1114 and 1118, before his accession to the throne, on the site associated with St Kentigern's cathedral of the sixth century. A rebuilt choir of which one tiny fragment survives is known to have been consecrated in 1197, and construction of a new nave was then started. Work on this was postponed, however, when Bishop William de Bondington decided to build an even grander choir — possibly to rival that of St Andrews, which was nearing completion around the mid-century. Work on Glasgow's choir probably started around 1240, when several gifts are recorded.

61. One of the capitals to the piers around the site of St Kentigern' tomb, in the crypt of Glasgow Cathedral. The mason's pleasure in carving this virtuoso display of stiff-leaf foliage is perhaps most evident in the way he has introduced a bird amongst the leaves.

Because of the fall of the land the choir had to be raised on a vaulted crypt. But, since this crypt was to contain the tomb of St Kentigern, it was not treated simply as an undercroft, but as a complex sequence of interlinked spaces defined by piers and vault formations. The two main foci of the crypt were the tomb of St Kentigern, and the Lady Chapel further east below the high altar in the choir. Emphasis on the former was subtly created by the formation of a canopy in the vaulting, supported by piers at the four corners, and on the latter by a wider canopy in the vaulting, occupying the full width of the central part of the crypt. The importance of the crypt is made particularly evident by the rather unusual siting of the Lady Chapel within it, and also by the high quality of the architectural detail. The stiff leaf capitals on the columns around St Kentigern's tomb are outstandingly fine, and bear comparison with the best work in England, at such as Lincoln Cathedral.

The design of the three-stage choir elevation on the upper level shows a skilful mixture of ideas found at a number of northern English buildings. The continuing influence of the choir of Lincoln Cathedral is apparent, although perhaps through the medium of more recent works, such as the Yorkshire Cistercian house of Rievaulx. However, Glasgow was never intended to have a high vault over the main body of the choir, unlike those churches, and the inner skin of the clerestory is consequently designed as a continuous arcade. Analogies for this may perhaps be sought in the choir of the Benedictine Abbey church of Whitby, in Yorkshire, where work was underway around the 1220s.

62. The choir of Glasgow Cathedral. One of the summits of achievement of Scottish Gothic architecture, Glasgow provides a fine demonstration of the aims of thirteenth century masons. The structural forces which hold up the complex building are suggested through a careful articulation of the elevations by means of a network of vertical and horizontal mouldings. Within this network each opening has its own unchangeable position, and an appearance of overall unity is given to the interior as a whole. Plane wall surfaces are reduced to a minimum, and seem almost like weightless membranes stretched across the skeletal frame.

a.   b.   c.   d.

63. A sketch which illustrates the emergence of plate tracery:

a. a pair of lancets
b. a pair of lancets within one window arch
c. a pair of lancets within one window arch, beneath which the plate of stone is pierced
d. one of the plate-traceried windows of Glasgow Cathedral choir.

64. The choir of Inchmahome Priory. It can be seen from this internal view that the impressive grouping of five tall lancets in the east wall is set within a single arch. Although no additional piercing was attempted at Inchmahome, it was perhaps a natural step to pierce the thin masonry between the lancet heads (see the window on the left in fig 62).

Glasgow has much of interest: the pointed timber ceiling, although heavily restored, shows how effectively such ceilings can give a sense of height to a building of modest scale, whilst the spatial complexity of the crypt is a rare Scottish reflection of an English taste emerging at this time. But one of the most fascinating features of Glasgow is the design of the choir aisle windows. In most early thirteenth century churches the windows were single or grouped lancets (tall pointed openings), as may be seen at the Augustinian priory churches of Restenneth in Angus, and Inchmahome on an island in the Lake of Mentieth. At the former there are singlet lancets to each bay of the choir flanks, and a group of three in the west wall. At Inchmahome, where the priory church was probably built soon after its foundation in about 1238, the east wall was pierced by a group of

five closely spaced and graded lancets, with the tallest at the centre. These lancets were embraced within a single arch, and it was an easy matter to pierce the thinner wall within such an arch by secondary openings above the lancet heads, creating what is known as plate tracery. This had already been done in the nave gallery of Jedburgh, and was also done in the choir triforium at Glasgow, although the idea was to be treated even more decoratively in Glasgow's choir aisles.

The next stage of this development in window design is to be seen at Dunblane, the other major cathedral under construction in the mid-thirteenth century. By 1233, when Clement was consecrated bishop of a diocese with a centre which fluctuated between Dunblane and Muthill, his diocese was in a state of disarray. After a papal mandate of 1237 ordered an investigation, its finances were reorganised, and the site of the cathedral was fixed at Dunblane. Shortly afterwards the lower walls of the entire new cathedral were laid out, incorporating a tower of the twelfth century from the earlier church which had occupied the site, and the various parts of the structure were built up to full height as funds became available. The earliest part to be completed was a range on the north

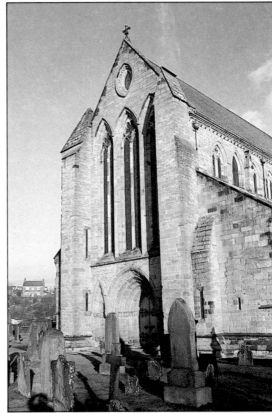

side of the choir for the chapter house, sacristy and treasury. The windows of this range were designed as groups of lancets within containing arches, and when the nave was started similar windows were provided in its flanking aisles. But there seems to have been a pause in this campaign, following which a modified design was adopted. There is some evidence that as originally designed the nave was to have had relatively low vaulted aisles, but that it was decided to build taller arcades, making no allowance for aisle vaults or any intermediate triforium stage. The two stage design which resulted has some analogies with such as the choir of Hedon church in eastern Yorkshire, although Dunblane is more finely finished.

A modified design for the clerestory of Dunblane was also introduced. In this some of the windows on the outer skin of the wall, and parts of the arcade along the inner face of the mural passage, were designed like the triforium arches of Glasgow, with paired lights within a containing arch, and a lesser light between the heads of the two; at Dunblane, however, more of the plate of stone between the light heads was opened up. This additional piercing reflects a development in tracery design first seen in the French cathedral of Reims in about 1210, from where it was

imported to Westminster Abbey in the 1240s. In tracery of the Reims type the openings are defined by curved bars of stone of uniform section, rather than left simply as voids in an area of masonry. At Dunblane the principle of the bars of stone seems to have been imperfectly understood, although the idea is seen properly applied in the transepts of Glasgow, which probably date from the later 1270s.

In the last decades of the thirteenth century two other important building campaigns were started, at Elgin and Sweetheart, in both of which the new type of tracery was used. At Elgin construction of a large three-towered cathedral was probably begun even before the see was moved to there from Spynie in 1224. This cathedral was extensively damaged by a fire in 1270 which necessitated much rebuilding, and led to a campaign of enlargement. The transepts, western towers and parts of the choir and nave were retained from the earlier building; but the presbytery was extended and the choir enveloped by aisles, whilst outer aisles were added along each side of the existing nave aisles and a frontispiece was raised between the two western towers. Additionally, an octagonal chapter house was built on the north side of the choir. Of all this work the best preserved is the

65. The nave of Dunblane Cathedral. The plan of the cathedral was set out in one campaign, but the various parts were only completed as funds became available. The nave was probably built around the third quarter of the thirteenth century, and its design appears to have been altered in the course of construction. After being roofless for about three centuries after the Reformation, the nave was restored in 1889-93 (see fig 92).

66. The west front of Dunblane Cathedral. With its elaborately moulded processional entrance, and triplet of traceried windows, this front provides a fine termination to the nave. The tracery represents a significant transitional stage in the history of Scottish tracery design.

new presbytery. Its plan (fig 10) is similar to St Andrews and Arbroath in the way the central part projects beyond the aisles to give prominence to the position of the high altar, and the east wall, with its tiers of grouped lancets, is also in the tradition of St Andrews and Arbroath. But at Elgin there are five rather than three lancets to each tier and within these windows simple bar tracery of the new type was constructed.

The finest surviving windows erected in this first phase of bar tracery are in the eastern parts of Sweetheart Abbey; fine examples were also inserted in the course of the continuing work at Glasgow Cathedral, but since they have been heavily augmented during nineteenth century restoration it is preferable to concentrate on those of Sweetheart. Founded in 1273 by Devorgilla, the mother of the future King John Balliol, Sweetheart was the last Cistercian abbey to be established in Scotland. In its design Cistercian austerity is maintained in the plan (fig 25), which is still essentially the same as at the earlier Cistercian churches, and also in the absence of a triforium. At English Cistercian houses — and also in the Scottish church at Newbattle, dedicated in 1233 — more complex planning had been accepted

67. The east front of Elgin Cathedral. Elgin may be seen as the culmination of the tradition of presbytery facade design which relied on tiers of grouped windows for its chief impact, and which had earlier been seen at St Andrews and Arbroath. In this case the greater number of windows in each tier, and the massive octagonal buttresses create a particularly satisfying design.

68. The abbey of Sweetheart from the south-east. The emphasis on the presbytery, in this otherwise rather austere Cistercian abbey church, is most marked in the great size of its traceried windows. In deference to the earlier ban on bell towers in Cistercian churches, it will be seen that the tower here barely rose above the roof line — the crow-stepped cap-house is a later addition.

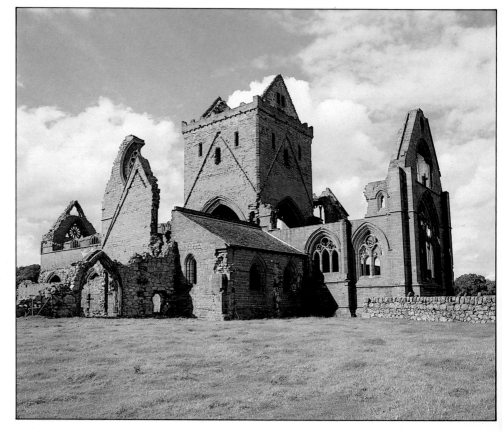

48

considerably before this date; yet at Sweetheart the only concessions to a less rigorous outlook are the squat crossing tower and some limited elaboration of detail, which is most obvious in the windows of the presbytery. In the earliest bar tracery the basic unit had been a simple combination of two lights within a containing arch, with a circlet between the light heads, although it was soon appreciated that interesting permutations could be made on this unit, as may be seen in the east window at Sweetheart. The master mason also showed knowledge of more recent types of tracery in which circlets were spread throughout the tracery field, and there was no grouping of the individual lights within subarches. This type of tracery had been developed in France in the 1230s, and taken up in England about twenty years later.

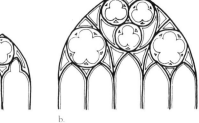

a.　　　　　　　　　b.　　　　　　　　　c.

69. Examples of tracery from the presbytery of Sweetheart Abbey:

a. shows the simplest type of bar tracery, with a circlet between two light heads

b. is the great east window which, whilst giving an impression of complexity, is simply a permutation on the theme of two lights and a circlet

c. shows the impact of new ideas in the way in which the circlets are fitted in between the light heads and the window arch.

The First Phase of Late Gothic

14TH AND EARLIER 15TH CENTURY

The relatively settled political conditions, which had encouraged so much building in the twelfth and thirteenth centuries, were shattered by the consequences of Edward I's treatment of Scotland after the deaths of Alexander III and his granddaughter. Edward's direct rule of Scotland from June 1291, and his judgement in favour of John Balliol as king in November of 1292, were followed by interference which forced Scotland into armed reaction and a renewed alliance with France in 1295. Inevitably, the major ecclesiastical building operations then in progress, including those at Glasgow, Elgin and Sweetheart were postponed for a long period.

This pause was of critical importance for the later history of Scottish ecclesiastical architecture, because it was in these same years that radical changes were being introduced by English masons which were to re-direct the course of architecture in England for the rest of the Middle Ages. Although from the earlier thirteenth century onwards there had probably been a growing pool of native masons in the Lowland areas of Scotland, who were competent to design and direct major operations, they had been heavily dependent on England for ideas, and their architecture can still only be understood within a northern British context. But the loss of contact with England after 1295 meant that Scottish masons had little chance of maintaining familiarity with the rapidly changing ideas of their English counterparts, and their eventual ability to catch up on lost ground was greatly impaired. For much of the fourteenth century ecclesiastical building

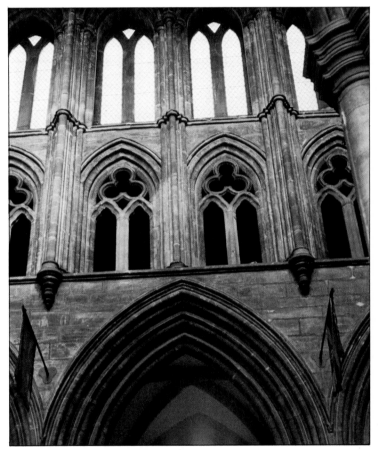

70. The nave of Glasgow Cathedral. The design of this part of Glasgow Cathedral has few parallels for the way in which the triforium is set back within arches which interconnect both triforium and clerestory. The design was partly conditioned by an operation of rebuilding which was started in the first half of the thirteenth century but which was left unfinished when attention moved to the choir. Work on the nave is likely to have re-started in the later thirteenth century, and to have continued sporadically over an extended period.

was sporadic. Royal gifts to Dunfermline in 1329 probably allowed the construction of its refectory to go ahead (fig 23), whilst the choir of Dunkeld was remodelled by Bishop Sinclair before his death in 1337. It is also possible that work on the nave of Glasgow Cathedral was continued during the century, to a plan dictated by the earlier false start, and with an unusual elevation in which the inter-

71. The presbytery and transepts of Melrose Abbey. Rebuilding of Melrose was started in the last decades of the fourteenth century, to a magnificent design which proved impossible to carry through to completion. The first phase of the new work appears to have been designed by English masons, possibly drawn from eastern Yorkshire.

linked triforium and clerestory have few parallels. However, those buildings at which work was in progress are too few and too disparate to allow any coherent picture of architectural attitudes in the fourteenth century to be gained.

It is only in the last decade of the century that the picture becomes clearer, and probably the most important building to be started at this time was the Cistercian abbey church of Melrose, which had been founded by David I around 1136. The church had been destroyed by English troops in 1385, but in 1389 Richard II contributed to its rebuilding, and the first parts to be designed appeared to promise a renewed reliance on English architectural guidance. As at Sweetheart, of more than a century earlier, the absence of a triforium and the simple plan were still in the early Cistercian tradition; but the magnificent east end, with its vast window and array of niches across the gable and buttresses, is related to English designs, such as that of the somewhat earlier collegiate church of Howden in eastern Yorkshire. However, Melrose marks a positive advance in its design of a grid-like pattern of rectilinear tracery to the east window, in the use of which it was in step with the most recent English ideas. Indeed, the east end

provides a significant stage in the development of northern English facade design which is otherwise unrepresented south of the Border.

However, before the choir and transepts were completed there was a marked change in the design which must mean that another mason from a different source had assumed control. This change is seen most clearly in the great south transept window and in the windows of the earlier of the chapels ranged along the south side of the nave aisle, where tracery of curvilinear rather than rectilinear patterns was employed. Tracery in which the component elements are defined by sinuously curved lines had been developed in England in the first decades of the fourteenth century, although it was later abandoned in favour of rectilinear designs; similar tracery was eventually adopted throughout much of northern Europe, where it was to remain in use for the rest of the Middle Ages. The use of such tracery in the second phase of the work at Melrose therefore suggests that its mason was either looking to outdated English models — or was looking beyond England.

We are fortunate at Melrose that the master mason of one phase of the protracted building operation left a record of his name and other works in an inscription. His name was John Morow, and since one of the most significant parts of the record he left is a statement that he had been born in Paris, it is tempting to speculate if he had travelled to Scotland in search of work at a time when the disruptions of the Hundred Years War were still limiting architectural opportunities in France. On the basis of this inscription there is some reason for attributing the rejection of English architectural guidance at Melrose to the intervention of a mason with personal knowledge of French architecture, and this provides a valuable indicator of one direction that church building in Scotland was now to take. England was no longer to be regarded as the only guide in matters of design, because Scottish patrons and masons were now prepared to look further afield for ideas. In the later fourteenth and early fifteenth century links with France were particularly close: the alliance between two countries had been renewed in 1391 and again in 1428, and in the latter year the marriage of the daughter of James I to the heir to the throne of France was arranged.

It is thus hardly surprising that France should have been a natural alternative source of guidance at this

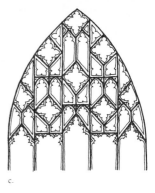

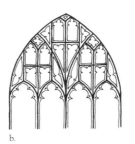

a. b. c.

72. Examples of tracery from the presbytery of Melrose Abbey. The rectilinear patterns of tracery seen in these windows provide the most obvious evidence that the first phase of remodelling was under English direction.

time, and at Melrose the results of this may be associated with a short phase of work which produced architecture of remarkable elegance, particularly in the first two nave chapels. This elegance is most apparent in the window tracery, where a fine combination of curvilinear with more regular figures is to be seen, which relates closely with the products of a brief period of French tracery design, as in the Lagrange Chapel at Amiens Cathedral of about 1373.

73. The earlier chapels on the south side of Melrose Abbey nave. In the two right-hand chapels, the first to be built, the windows are filled with tracery which, despite the damage it has suffered, can be seen to be of marked elegance.

74. The collegiate church of Lincluden, from the south-east. Set in Nithsdale, Lincluden may be the 'Nyddysdayl' which is included amongst the list of his works which the mason John Morow left at Melrose. The restrained elegance of the choir of this church is strikingly akin to that of the first south nave chapels at Melrose.

Morow's inscription also includes a list of his other works and, although most of them have been lost, two may be identifiable. They are Lincluden collegiate church ("Nyddysdayl") and the Cluniac abbey of Paisley ("Paslay"), where the choir and north nave aisle respectively reveal a number of significant similarities to Melrose. Although none of these works can be dated with certainty, the weight of evidence points to the early decades of the fifteenth century for their construction. The clearest link between them all is the employment of similar moulded masonry details and tracery types, and if they are all indeed by the same mason, the most complete illustration of his abilities is seen in the choir of Lincluden.

Lincluden collegiate church was founded in 1389 within a suppressed Benedictine nunnery by Archibald, third Earl of Douglas, although it is unlikely that rebuilding was started before his death in 1400. The new choir was probably built by the fourth earl, who died in 1424, and his wife, Princess Margaret. That earl's exploits in France, which eventually earned him the dukedom of Touraine, doubtless gave him an appreciation of Gallic architectural sophistication, and encouraged him to emulate that quality in his family's church. The result

is a building which is permeated by a fine sense of elegance, but which is nevertheless clearly not French; it is also a building which still owes much to the early tradition of dependence on English architectural leadership, but is equally clearly not English. At Lincluden, and the growing number of other churches being produced at that time, a manner of design can be seen to be emerging which is, for the first time in the Middle Ages, identifiably Scottish in character. This character was to show considerable variety depending on the range of influences acting on it at any one time, but it was never again to be dominated from one direction.

Apart from its architecture Lincluden is also notable for the carved stone fixtures around the site of the high altar. To its north, in the position customarily taken by the builder of a church, is the magnificent tomb of Princess Margaret, who died in about 1456, with a heraldic display running along the arcaded base to proclaim her importance. Adjacent to this is a finely worked door into the sacristy. On the opposite side of the choir is a *piscina* in which the vessels used at mass were washed, and close to it are the *sedilia*, where the priest and his assistants sat at parts of the service. Such fixtures were to become more frequently a feature of the finer churches, although they were seldom designed with such attention to detail. The stone screen which enclosed the priests' choir also still stands, and a section of the timber choir stalls is preserved at the National Museum of Antiquities in Edinburgh.

In the last years of the fourteenth century, and the early years of the fifteenth, several other important building campaigns were started. One of these was at Elgin Cathedral, where major rebuilding was necessitated after Alexander Stewart, Earl of Buchan, had retaliated against Bishop Alexander Bur's excommunication of him by setting the town and cathedral on fire in 1390. The damage caused by the aptly named 'Wolf of Badenoch' was extensive, and repairs were in progress over a very long period. The most immediate repairs were probably to the presbytery and choir, and from the new windows placed in the choir aisles we can see that great care was taken to make the new work sit sympathetically with the old.

Ironically, tracery of a similar intersecting pattern was designed for the chapel at the east end of the south aisle added onto Fortrose Cathedral at about this time; traditionally this aisle was built by Euphemia, Countess of Ross, the wife of that Earl of Buchan who

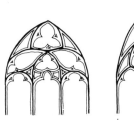 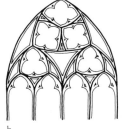

75. Examples of window tracery which may be attributable to John Morow:

a. is employed, with slight variations, at Melrose and Lincluden, and also at Paisley Abbey.
b. is found at Lincluden and Paisley, although in both cases it has been badly damaged.

a.　　　　　b.

76. Stone furnishings inside the choir of Lincluden Collegiate Church. On the left, within an unusually elaborate niche, is the *piscina*, for the washing of vessels used to contain the consecrated bread and wine at mass. To the right are the *sedilia*, on which the priest, deacon and subdeacon sat for parts of the service.

77. The cathedral of Fortrose, from the north-west. The principal surviving part was probably added to the cathedral by Euphemia, Countess of Ross, and the two eastern bays appear to have been intended for her burial place and chantry chapel. On the left in this view is a range which used to stand in a similar relationship to the choir as the sacristy and chapter house range at Dunblane (fig 6).

In the first decade of the fifteenth century another major building, the nave of Dunkeld Cathedral, was started. At Dunkeld we owe thanks to one of its canons, Alexander Myln, for writing a volume on the lives of its bishops which included their building activities. From this we know that the nave was started on 27 April 1406 by Bishop Robert de Cardeny, that it was dedicated by Bishop Thomas Lauder in 1464, and that the latter bishop also started to construct the adjacent tower. Dunkeld's seven-bay aisled nave is one of the most telling illustrations of Scotland's newly emerging architectural independence and its appearance, although handsome, is undoubtedly rather idiosyncratic. Its arcades, carried on squat cylindrical piers, open into aisles lit by finely traceried windows; but, although one of these aisles was stone-vaulted, the other had a timber ceiling. At triforium level in each bay there is a wide semi-circular opening subdivided into two smaller arches, whilst the clerestory has two-light windows of more conventional design. A noteworthy aspect of the building is the use of cylindrical piers, since such piers had been generally abandoned in the greater Scottish churches since the twelfth century, until being revived for use in a small number of late medieval churches. Significantly, the same period was to witness their renewed employment in several other parts of Europe, suggesting that the Scottish usage was a reflection of a continental fashion. Perhaps the closest analogies for the Scottish examples are to be found in the Low Countries.

In the later Middle Ages the Low Countries were the area with which Scotland had its closest trading links, whilst there were also strong diplomatic and cultural ties, and it is evident that the artistic products of that area were much admired in Scotland by those who could afford to buy them. There is thus every likelihood that, as Scottish masons and the patrons of building operations looked around for new architectural stimuli, they would become aware of ideas current in an area with which there were close contacts, and take from there whatever might seem attractive. The churches of the fifteenth and sixteenth centuries provide a number of examples of what appear to be borrowings from the architectural repertoire of the Low Countries, and it is possible that the arcade piers of Dunkeld are one example. Nevertheless, as with the borrowings from France at Melrose, there is no question of the end product looking as if it were a building in France or in the Low Countries. The process of seeking new ideas was a selective one in which the borrowed ideas were

78. The nave of Dunkeld Cathedral from the north-west. Although still with three stages to the internal elevation, like the major churches of the twelfth and thirteenth centuries, the early fifteenth century work at Dunkeld reveals a radically simplified approach to design. The complex articulation of wall faces, seen at such as Glasgow, has been abandoned in favour of a straightforward expression of surfaces which suggests that the master mason was looking to new sources of inspiration.

had devastated Elgin. It seems that the chapel was intended to house a chantry for its builder, because its eastern arch was designed to accommodate a handsome canopied tomb. Since the character of this work appears consistent with a date at the turn of the fourteenth and fifteenth centuries there is little reason to question that the Countess of Ross was indeed responsible for it. Apart from similarities of window design, the new work at Fortrose shows other links with the remodelled choir aisles at Elgin, including the design of the fine stone vaulting and the form of the buttresses. A building as magnificent as Elgin must, as a matter of course, have provided an inspiration for other churches in the area, but in the late fourteenth century an additional factor may have been that the bishop of Fortrose, Alexander de Kylwos, had earlier been dean of Elgin.

grafted onto the native stock, and by which the stock was enriched — but not overwhelmed.

Late Gothic

In the last century before the Reformation the balance of church building swung from the greater to the lesser churches. Although a number of major cathedral and abbey building campaigns which had been started earlier were to continue through much of the period, and minor works were undertaken at many greater foundations, there is evidence of few large-scale building operations being initiated within them. At the same time the pace of work on some of the continuing operations was slower than might have been expected and, indeed, at Melrose it seems that the rebuilding started so ambitiously at the end of the fourteenth century was never completed. One reason for this was that the lay folk were increasingly choosing to give to their parish churches the financiial support which earlier generations had lavished on the abbeys and cathedrals. The late Middle Ages is above all the age of the parish church, and this is supremely illustrated by the magnificent churches which were raised in the greater burghs. St Nicholas at Aberdeen, St Giles at Edinburgh, St Mary at Haddington, St Michael at Linlithgow, St John at Perth and Holy Rude at Stirling all give witness to the chief loyalty of the late medieval lay folk. These churches are outside the scope of this book, but the same picture is conveyed by many of the churches now in the care of the State.

One of the earlier examples of the new type of church which was to rise across the wealthier parts of the country is that of St Mary at Dunglass, in East Lothian. A chapel for the spiritual needs of the Home family and their dependents, with priests to pray for their souls, was on the site from at least the first quarter of the fifteenth century. But in the 1440s Sir Alexander Home decided to form the priests of the church into a college, and to reflect its new status the church was rebuilt. It was first laid out with a nave and smaller choir, with a projection on the north of the latter for use either as a sacristy or tomb chapel. But it was soon decided to add transepts and a central tower, and additional supports had to be inserted in the form of piers of masonry set a little awkwardly into the eastern end of the nave. Architecturally the church is severely

plain, with very little carved detail other than on the chancel arch caps and the canopies of the *sedilia*. In the rather rectilinear design of the windows there is a suggestion of awareness of contemporary English work; although, as if to counter this, the pointed barrel vaults which cover all parts of the church except the tower give the building a pronouncedly Scottish character. Vaults of this type, with an external roof of stone flags, were to become a characteristic feature of the more costly late Gothic churches of Scotland.

Similar vaults were built over the choir and transepts added by successive Lords Seton to the parish church close to their castle at Seton, and within which they lavishly endowed a college. A detailed account of the family's building operations was written by Sir

79. The collegiate church of Dunglass from the north. To the left is the choir, from which a sacristy or chapel projects; to the right of the tower and transepts is the nave.

80. The collegiate church of Seton. The apse of the collegiate choir is in the foreground, with the transepts and tower beyond. The eastern walls of the transepts were left unpierced to accommodate carved retables behind the altars.

including a canopied tomb, a *piscina* and a recess which may be either *sedilia* or a credence shelf (for the display of items to be used in the mass). By comparison with Dunglass, Seton gives an impression of greater structural lightness, because the ratio of window to wall is much greater, with consequently less sense of being overwhelmed by the sheer mass of masonry in the walls and vaults. In its choir and transepts are good examples of the type of window tracery that was by then favoured in Scotland's more generously endowed late medieval churches. Most of the windows are of two or three lights, with pairs of curved dagger-like figures bending in towards a central figure at the window apex. In the end walls of the transepts, where the vaults allowed larger windows, there are four-light permutations on this theme, with additional figures between the sub-arches.

An immediate source for the basic design of Seton may have been the chapel Bishop Kennedy built for his college of St Salvator at St Andrews, which was founded in 1450. Both St Salvator and Seton were aisle-less rectangular structures with a polygonal eastern apse (and both were designed to be covered by a pointed barrel vault). However, the ultimate inspiration for such planning may have been the many private or academic chapels of similar size and plan built in France from the thirteenth century onwards. The relatively inexpensive spatial sophistication which could be gained by using this type of plan gave it a considerable following in late medieval Scotland for many types of church, and one of its most pleasing expressions is the unvaulted choir of the Cluniac abbey of Crossraguel, in Ayrshire.

Richard Maitland in the mid-sixteenth century, which recorded that it was George, first Lord Seton, who planned the college and built much of the choir before his death in about 1478, although the necessary papal approval was only received in 1492. In the sixteenth century Lady Janet, widow of the third Lord Seton, added the transepts and tower between the newly completed choir and the old nave, in order to accommodate altars for additional priests.

In its final state Seton had one of the most splendid of Scotland's collegiate choirs, and particular emphasis was concentrated on the presbytery by making its eastern end a polygonal apse with an attractive surface application of decorative ribs to the vault over that area. As at Lincluden the east end was also enriched by a display of finely sculptured fixtures,

Crossraguel is one of the few abbeys to have rebuilt its choir at this time, and the scale of the work is relatively small. The choir and adjoining range on the east side of the cloister were set out in one campaign (fig 12), as may be seen from the continuity of the lower walling beneath both of them; but there are signs of building pauses which suggest that even work on such a modest scale was stretching the abbey's resources. Traditionally the work is ascribed to the abbacy of Colin, between about 1460 and 1490, but, whilst a date in that period may be appropriate for the completion of the east range, the choir could have been started earlier. The way in which the choir interior is regulated vertically into bays by wall shafts, and horizontally by string courses below the windows and around their heads, reveals the presence of a mason of high calibre.

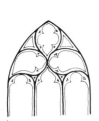
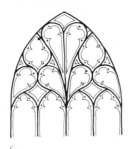

a.   b.   c.

82. A sketch of the varieties of tracery at Seton collegiate church. By means of comparatively simple combinations of curvilinear tracery forms, pleasingly rich designs could be built up. Similar tracery was to be found in several other Scottish churches of the period.

83. The choir of Crossragual Abbey Church. Externally this choir would have had a similar appearance to that of Seton, before the loss of its roof and the tracery within its windows.

84. The lower chapel at Restalrig. It is now rather difficult to understand how this extraordinary little building was intended to be used, although it is possible that its centralised design was suggested by some use in connection with a sacred spring.

The presence of an ingenious mason is also apparent in the extraordinary design of the two-storeyed hexagonal chapel built onto the side of the church of Restalrig under the patronage of James III, which was nearing completion in 1487 when a college was founded within it. Scottish masons of the second half of the fifteenth century appear to have taken a renewed interest in the problems of constructing stone vaults over centralised structures, although their designs show no real advance on what had already been achieved in the polygonal chapter houses of the thirteenth century. In the lower chapel at Restalrig the hexagonal vault springs from a central six-shafted pier, and similarly the octagonal vault reconstructed within Elgin chapter house by Bishop Andrew Stewart (1482-1501) also rests on a central pier. However, from surviving fragments it seems that the upper vault at Restalrig may have been slightly more adventurous in that it dispensed with the support of a central pier, as had been the case in the early thirteenth century chapter house at Inchcolm. Two other inter-related structures which may be mentioned at this point, on account of their superficial visual similarities with Restalrig and Elgin, are the chapter house in the east range of Crossraguel, and that at the Cistercian abbey of Glenluce. Both of

these buildings, although square in plan, give something of the same appearance as Restalrig and Elgin from the way in which the four compartments of the vault rest on a central pier; however, the immediate inspiration for their design may have been the upper chapter house at Glasgow cathedral, which had been remodelled to a similar form in the second quarter of the fifteenth century by Bishop John Cameron.

In passing, reference should be made to the caps at several of these buildings which are decorated by foliage carving of the slightly stereotyped form which may be aptly compared to seaweed. In general, although with honourable exceptions, decorative sculture at this period was less inventive than it had been in the twelfth and thirteenth centuries: it seems that the master masons in charge of design may have come to expect greater overall control of building operations, with a consequent reduction of individual initiative for the hewing masons.

The cost of constructing the stone vaults which covered most of these buildings could be afforded by relatively few patrons, and many of the churches rebuilt to accommodate colleges of priests for Scotland's greater families were consequently built to designs which were in general little different from the lesser parish churches. Nevertheless, we know from the rare survivals of paintings and furnishings at the Angus church of St Marnock at Fowlis Easter, which was rebuilt in 1453 for a college founded by Lord Gray, that even an unassuming rectangular church might contain some excellent works of religious art. At the Banffshire church of Deskford, for example, a very plain building still retains an elaborately carved

85. The interior of the chapter house of Glenluce Abbey. This square structure is vaulted in four smaller square compartments, which spring from the central pier. Despite lacking the finesse of the best buildings of the period, its details, such as the deep base and angled faces of the cap to the central pier, are characteristic of Scottish Late Gothic work. The remains of the tiled floor, and the bench on which the monks sat at their chapter meetings, are valuable survivals.

86. One of the carved caps of the door into Glenluce Abbey chapter house. The rather stereotyped foliage carving includes some of the type often likened to seaweed.

sacrament house in which the consecrated sacrament could be contained with appropriate dignity.

At Innerpeffray, in Perthshire, the church was rebuilt by John, Lord Drummond, around the first decade of the sixteenth century for a college which had grown from the endowment of a number of priests. As at Fowlis Easter, it was a rectangular building — although with a projecting sacristy on its north side — but the interior of the church is more complex than might be expected from its shape. Near the western end an arch defines a vestibule area, within which a spiral stair leads up to a post-Reformation 'laird's loft', and it is not inconceivable that there may have been an earlier family pew in this position. There was a further but more orthodox subdivision about half-way down the church, where corbels (projecting blocks of stone) indicate the site of the loft on the rood screen dividing collegiate choir from nave. Additional altars were sometimes placed on these lofts and, if the church had an organ, it may have been here.

The church built by Sir David Murray at Tullibardine in Perthshire, before his death in 1452, was probably also originally of rectangular plan. As at Innerpeffray it seems that Sir David proposed to found a college, although there is no evidence it was ever formally established. Nevertheless, additional priests were added to the original complement, and the church was eventually enlarged to a cruciform plan with a small western tower. The unbuttressed walls of the church were clearly never intended to carry a vault, and instead a timber roof was constructed, which survives in a partly restored state. Certain details suggest that the roof structure was intended to be concealed by a timber boarded ceiling, which would then presumably have been painted. On heraldic evidence the work of enlargement was probably undertaken in the lifetime of Sir Andrew Murray, a younger son of the family, and his wife, Margaret Barclay, who were married at a date around 1500. A date in the early sixteenth century for the enlarge-ment is supported by the form of the tracery in the windows of the two transepts. This tracery is essen-tially of common types in late medieval Scotland, except that there are none of the spur-like cusps which were usually employed to elaborate the shapes defined by the curved tracery bars. Simplified tracery like this may probably be regarded as another borrowing from the Low Countries, where the brick construction of many windows encouraged the rejec-tion of unnecessary detail from the later fifteenth century onwards.

87. The interior of the collegiate church at Innerpeffray, looking westwards. Some of the corbels which supported the loft above the rood screen may be seen in the side walls, as may one of the inscribed consecration crosses which marked the positions at which the bishop sprinkled holy water at the consecration of the church. There may have been a pew for the founder of the college within the arch at the west end of the church.

88. Interior of the church of Tullibardine, looking eastwards. The high altar was against the east wall, which was left blank to accommodate a reredos; additional altars were in the transepts, into which the arch on each side opened.

89. The polygonal north chapel of the church of the Dominican friars at St Andrews. The precise relationship of this chapel to the body of the church is no longer known, but it is likely that it formed a transeptal projection. The loop-like tracery designs of the large windows suggests that the mason was aware of architectural developments in the Low Countries, but in other respects the architecture is closely akin to such as Seton church.

90. Examples of tracery employing loop-like patterns: a. is from the transepts added onto the church of Tullibardine at a date around 1500   b. and c. are from the St Andrews church of the Dominican friars.

Closely related tracery is to be seen in a number of other Scottish buildings, including the polygonal chapel which originally projected from the north side of the church of the Dominican Friars at St Andrews. This fragment, which is one of the few examples of mendicant architecture to survive in Scotland, was built about 1516, when the Dominicans agreed to devote to that purpose money left by Bishop Elphinstone of Aberdeen. It is even a possibility that this church could have been one of the vehicles by which such simplified loop-like tracery was introduced into Scotland from the Low Countries, since the Scottish Dominican Province had close contacts with that of the Low Countries.

The advanced ideas seen in major buildings like the St Andrews Dominican church had little impact in peripheral regions such as the Western Highlands, which still tended to pursue an independent course owing as much to Ireland as to Lowland Scotland. One of the most fascinating products of this meeting of two cultures is the early sixteenth century church of St Clement at Rodel, at the southern tip of Harris. It is an unusually ambitious church for this part of Scotland, and undoubtedly owed much to the influence of the abbey at Iona, where Abbot Dominic had begun a major remodelling in the mid-fifteenth century. It was built to a cruciform plan, with a western tower on an elevated rock outcrop at the west end. Within the church the transept arches and eastern window show some attempt at architectural refinement which was clearly inspired by Iona. But the main focus of the choir is undoubtedly the arched tomb of Alexander MacLeod of Dunvegan, which he built in 1528, nearly twenty years before his death. The arch and back panel are decorated by fascinating illustrations of some of the important things in the life of a great man of the western seaboard (including a galley, a castle and a hunting scene), and by religious images which give little hint of impending changes.

91. The church of St Clement at Rodel. This fine cruciform structure, which is the most ambitious medieval church in the Western Isles apart from Iona, may incorporate parts of an earlier building. The form of the church as we now see it is probably attributable to Alexander MacLeod of Dunvegan, who built a handsome tomb for himself on the south side of the choir in 1528.

SCOTTISH CHURCHES AND THE REFORMATION

Although the Scottish Reformation was accomplished in 1560, when the mass and papal authority were formally abolished by Parliament, the urge for reform had been gathering momentum in some quarters for several years. As early as the 1540's sermons were being preached against soul masses, for example, whilst the declining fervour of monastic life was a major cause for concern. Nevertheless, to many of those living in the mid-sixteenth century it can have been by no means certain that Scotland would follow England and some of the German States in breaking with Rome. By that time the signs that the Church was beginning to face the abuses which beset it were being confirmed by the Council of Trent, and the call for Counter-Reformation was already gathering strength.

The Stewart monarchs adopted an ambivalent role towards the Church in the later Middle Ages. Whilst professing a desire to see an improvement in the state of the monasteries, for example, in the later fifteenth century James IV had begun a process of appointing commendators as heads of many of them, rather than abbots or priors who were professed to the monastic life. By doing so he was able to reward kinsmen or favoured individuals at no cost to himself, although few of those he imposed on the monasteries had any interest in improving the quality of religious life. On the contrary, many of them were sufficiently astute to have their office made effectively hereditary, and ultimately succeeded in retaining the lands of the monasteries for their families after the Reformation.

92. Dunblane Cathedral in the late seventeenth century. By this date the nave was already roofless and falling into decay, the parishioners having converted the more conveniently planned choir to meet their reformed needs. To provide sufficient seating galleries were inserted, the stair to one of which may be seen at the east end of the choir. (*From John Slezer*, Theatrum Scotiae, 1693)

93. The abbey of Arbroath in the late seventeenth century. Perhaps the most surprising thing to be shown by this view is that the abbey had declined to almost its present state of advanced ruination in less than one and a half centuries, showing how rapid was the decay once the roof and glazing were removed. (*From John Slezer*, Theatrum Scotiae, 1693)

At the Reformation the fate of the church buildings varied considerably. The majority of parish churches were simple structures which were relatively easily adapted to new forms of worship, and in any case the financial position of the reformed Church was so unstable for many years that it was not able to contemplate much new building. It was only much later that most of the simpler churches were replaced by buildings of greater architectural pretensions. At most of the larger churches (including several of the cathedrals which had also served parishes) the structure was either divided into two or even three separate churches, or only part of the building was retained in use. However, in a number of parishes it was decided to take over a monastic church for parochial worship in preference to the existing parish church, as happened at Culross, although in most cases only a part of the building was kept in repair.

Accurate estimates of the damage caused to other types of churches at the Reformation are difficult to achieve. The friaries suffered more directly than most because the begging life of the communities was unpopular once their original fervour had waned, whilst their urban settings also made them vulnerable to an inflamed populace. In the monastic churches,

some of which had already suffered from English attacks in 1544 and 1547, the chief targets tended to be the fixtures and furnishings associated with the old forms of worship, rather than the buildings themselves. Yet, once the windows had been destroyed, a process of long-term deterioration was already instigated which was frequently accelerated by the theft of the roof covering. At many monasteries it was in the interest of the commendators to keep part of the domestic buildings intact for their own residence. At Ardchattan, for example, the descendants of the commendators still occupy a house which incorporates part of the domestic buildings of the priory. In some cases the secularised residue of the monastic community also continued to occupy parts of the buildings until death took its final toll. Nevertheless, those monastic churches which were not to be put to parochial uses soon proved to be irresistible quarries of building materials.

As with monastic churches, it was the trappings of the cathedrals which attracted the main indignation of the reformers, whilst the buildings were less subject to systematic attack. However, although the office of bishop was retained for many years, its function for much of the time was reduced to little more than that of a superintending minister, and thus most of the

94. Elgin Cathedral from the south in 1826. From the later eighteenth century onwards the greater medieval buildings came to be seen as objects worthy of interest, and a movement grew up to preserve what had survived. At Elgin a keeper of the ruins was appointed in 1825 who — virtually single-handed — cleared the ruins of rubble. The keeper, John Shanks, is shown seated on a tombstone in the foreground of this view which celebrates the newly re-discovered beauty of the cathedral. (*From* A series of views . . . of Elgin Cathedral, 1826)

distinctive functions of a cathedral as a bishop's church were removed. At both Elgin and St Andrews the cathedrals were deserted in favour of the more conveniently sized parish church. Elsewhere the cathedrals were either modified for parochial use or simply abandoned; exceptionally, at Glasgow and Kirkwall, the parishioners expanded to occupy the whole building, and not just those parts which had previously been devoted to parochial worship.

The Scottish Reformation may also be seen to represent almost as much of a break with the architectural, as with the religious past. The unavoidable lack of any concerted building programme by the reformed Church came at a period when changed architectural forms were gaining increased acceptance, and when new building did eventually become more widely possible the resultant churches usually had a rather different architectural veneer from those produced previously. That is not to say that the ideas offered by such a radically innovative church as that at Burntisland in Fife, of 1592, found an immediate following, and for many years a high proportion of those churches built were of the same rectangular plan as most medieval churches. Indeed, in cases where the patron's sympathies were conservative, even the architectural veneer of the past might be copied, as in the Fife church of Dairsie, which was built by Archbishop Spottiswoode in 1621. But, allowing for all reservations, it is still essentially true that the Reformation marks an end to the main stream of medieval ecclesiastical architecture, and when on occasions its forms were re-used it was because of their connotations rather than because they were a part of a continuing tradition.

One long-term consequence of the Reformation for many of the abbeys and cathedrals followed from James VI's Act of Annexation of 1587, by which he claimed the estates of the bishops and monasteries on the grounds that the original endowments had been made from the resources of the Crown. His claim was only partly successful, since the hold of many commendators on their monastic lands was too firm to dislodge, and James was prudent enough to buy the support of other adherents by the grant of Church lands along with appropriate ennoblement. However, the act was to give the Crown the nominal ownership of many ecclesiastical buildings, and this was to become important two centuries later.

The Crown ownership of these buildings was generally disregarded until interest in them as objects of picturesque and archaeological curiosity began to emerge from the later eighteenth century onwards. As early as 1789 the Barons of the Exchequer were persuaded to pay for necessary repairs to the church of St Rule at St Andrews, and by the 1830's the government was beginning to accept a positive role in the preservation and presentation of those ecclesiastical buildings — whether in use or ruinous — which could be shown to be Crown property. This tendency was given further impetus by the passing of the Ancient Monuments Acts of 1882 and 1900, which allowed the State to take important archaeological and architectural relics of the past into its care. As a result in Scotland there are now over eighty ecclesiastical monuments, or monuments with a significant ecclesiastical element, which are maintained by the State and open to the public.

Index

Suggestions for Further Reading and Reference

G W S Barrow, *The kingdom of the Scots*, 1973.

Christopher Brooke, *The monastic world*, 1974.

Ian Cowan, *The parishes of medieval Scotland*, 1967.

Ian Cowan and David Easson, *Medieval religiou houses, Scotland*, 2nd ed 1976.

Ian Cowan, 'The medieval Church in Scotland: select critical bibliography', *Records of the Scottis Church history society*, vol 21, 1981.

Stewart Cruden, *Scottish abbeys*, 1960.

Gordon Donaldson, *Scotland, Church and Natio through sixteen centuries*, 2nd ed 1972.

John Dowden, *The medieval Church in Scotland*, 1910

A A M Duncan, *Scotland, the making of the kingdom* 1975.

David Knowles, *The monastic order in England*, 2nd ed 1963.

David MacGibbon and Thomas Ross, *The ecclesi astical architecture of Scotland*, 1896-7.

Peter McNeill and Ranald Richolson, *An historica atlas of Scotland c400-c1600*, 1975.

Ranald Nicholson, *Scotland, the later middle ages* 1974.

R W Southern, *Western society and the Church in th middle ages*, 1970.

Geoffrey Webb, *Architecture in Britain, the middle ages* 2nd ed 1965.

Christopher Wilson, entries on medieval churches in Colin McWilliam (ed), *Buildings of Scotland*, 1978-